Creating the Trusted Team of Advisers for a Family Business

Author
Ken McCracken

Managing director
Sian O'Neill

Creating the Trusted Family Team of Advisers for a Family Business
is published by

Globe Law and Business Ltd
3 Mylor Close
Horsell
Woking
Surrey GU21 4DD
United Kingdom
Tel: +44 20 3745 4770
www.globelawandbusiness.com

Printed and bound by CPI Group (UK) Ltd, Croydon CR0 4YY

Creating the Trusted Family Team of Advisers for a Family Business

ISBN 9781787422209
EPUB ISBN 9781787422216
Adobe PDF ISBN 9781787422223
Mobi ISBN 9781787422230

Table of contents

Introduction

This special report addresses the persistence of an idea that is sustained by a combination of the self-interest of its proponents and the current absence of a viable alternative. The idea is that every family business needs an adviser who is trusted above others and who can do things for the family and its business that presumably other advisers cannot be trusted to do. Meet the individual trusted adviser, or most trusted adviser.

The term 'family business' is used in this report to describe any group of relatives from the first generation onwards who own a business. The family could be any of the following:

- a nuclear family of parents and children;
- a blended family of partners and children from more than one relationship;
- a multi-generational family or network of families descended from a known ancestor; or
- a family that extends beyond blood relatives to include those with other kinship ties.

In whatever way a family defines its connections, some members have ownership control of a business either directly or through other entities such as trusts, partnerships or holding companies that are in turn controlled by the family. The family might also manage its business or could have hired non-family to take care of this.

The 'familiness' of the business is fixed whenever the intention of the current owners becomes to pass control to the next generation of their family. This intention may have been the aim when the owners started or took over the business, or may have become a goal as they grew older and the question of "What next?" could no longer be ignored. Until this intention forms, the owners are living another dream – one which is about being in control of their own venture and which may include broader aims of making a fortune, building a reputation, creating employment, putting something back into society and simply trying to be happy.

When the current owners start thinking about the "What next?", they will be concerned about the relationships among family members and the interaction between the family members and their business. At this time, potentially sensitive questions demand attention, such as who in the family will be the future owners or the next leaders of the business. While some families figure out how to balance the demands of the business with their desire to be fair, loving and considerate to family members, others seek help from advisers.

Since our experience of trusting – for good or ill – starts with family and grows out to others, most family businesses and advisers share a natural instinct towards forming a trust-based relationship of some sort. The notion of there being an individual adviser who can be trusted to look after the family and its business can be traced back to the major-domo – who, incidentally, could claim to have been providing family office services long before the term came into vogue. In time, the major-domo became known as the general practitioner – someone who could look after a family's personal and commercial interests; but nowadays the general practitioner has become extinct and specialists dominate the advisory space.

Specialists seek to understand the complex reality of a family business by deconstructing it into a series of specialist problems to which there are technical answers. This is accepted because nowadays every adviser is some sort of specialist; but the families might reasonably question whether life is really that simple. This reductive approach also means that families are left with the challenge of pulling together different advice from various specialists, which is awkward when they lack the technical know-how that is needed for the task. So the family might prefer to delegate this role to one of their advisers who, as well as being a specialist, is generally trusted by the family.

These individual and most trusted advisers are often described as a

"Specialists seek to understand the complex reality of a family business by deconstructing it into a series of specialist problems to which there are technical answers. This is accepted because nowadays every adviser is some sort of specialist; but the families might reasonably question whether life is really that simple."

species of specialists who possess soft skills that enable them to develop strong personal relationships with the owners and leaders who are currently in power. It is true that business families often seek advice when emotions resulting from anxiety about a particular situation, or the future in general, become sufficient to prompt action; and in such situations, soft skills or emotional intelligence will be very useful for the adviser and helpful to the family. However, do soft skills plus a specialism explain everything about the role of a trusted adviser?

In order to be seen to offer more, an adviser might be tempted to tell the family business client about best practices in relation to how to organise its business and family life. Indeed, the terms 'trusted adviser' and 'best practice' are often found in close proximity, as though one of the tests of a trusted adviser is being someone who can be trusted to know what is best for the family and its business.

The description of a trusted adviser could therefore be a specialist who possesses soft skills to a degree absent in other advisers and who can be trusted to recommend some best practices for the family and its business. These advisers also help to pull together the advice from other specialists, who presumably have to come to terms with being a sub-species of less trusted adviser.

However, there are problems with the individual trusted adviser as a business model:

- It puts a lot of power in one adviser's hands, which some families will dislike. This power is reflected in the term 'gatekeeper' which is used as a synonym for the trusted adviser, whom the family and other advisers must pass through in order to meet and work together.
- If trusted adviser status is based on strong personal relationships with those in the family and the business who are currently in power, it implies that becoming a trusted adviser involves growing old with the generation that currently controls the business.
- The trusted adviser is thus likely to be of an older age and to be more aligned to the senior generation in a family business than to the next generation, which might not be liked by the latter.
- This creates succession problems for the adviser, his or her host organisation and the family business. It makes it difficult to train younger advisers to become trusted early in their careers, which makes it more challenging for them to take over this role when they become older.

The model of the individual trusted adviser in truth is not much use for building sustainable trust relationships that can transcend the generational changes that will happen in every family business and in the adviser's business. The focus on an individual relationship also obscures powerful elements in the decision by a family business and an adviser to trust each other. Economic necessity and competence will have an impact on the relationship. Trust will also be affected by the role of organisations, rather than individuals, and especially the ways in which they market or promote their desire to be perceived as trusted advisers.

Persisting with the idea of an individual trusted adviser seems to be trying to move the relationship between advisers and family businesses forward by looking backwards – nostalgically, perhaps – to the era of the major-domo or general practitioner, adapted to take account of the current dominance of specialisms. Reaching for best practices does not do much to improve this model, as these are often excessive generalisations from selected examples that reduce complex family businesses to facile slogans that are then falsely presented as universal laws.

To move forward in an era when every adviser is a specialist, it is necessary to explore an alternative to the individual trusted adviser. This special report describes how the trusted adviser for a family business could be a high-performing, inter-disciplinary advisory team, probably from different organisations, with demonstrably effective processes for looking after an entire family and its business interests. The members of this team are committed to helping the family achieve whatever success means for it, in terms of both family and business life; and as in a true team, the individual reward for each adviser is to some extent dependent on the other team members.

This level of commitment to the team and the family business is greater than the type of advisory team that already exists, where a multi-disciplinary group of specialists form a team out of necessity in order to execute a particular transaction. In this type of team there is a minimum of interdependence among specialists beyond where their technical worlds overlap or collide.

High-performance teams are used in several areas of commerce, sports, science and the arts, so why not among advisers who serve family businesses? The immediate response is likely to be, "It will not be easy"; or even more assertively, "It will never work." These reactions are based on the view that it would be too challenging for a group of ambitious, self-motivated advisers with different specialisms from separate organisations to come together and form a high-performing team. However, the inter-disciplinary team model is about progress and progress is never easy. Also, surely moving forward towards this

"High-performance teams are used in several areas of commerce, sports, science and the arts, so why not among advisers who serve family businesses? The immediate response is likely to be, 'It will not be easy'; or even more assertively, 'It will never work.'"

model is likely to be no more difficult than trying to execute the awkward manoeuvre of moving forwards by looking backwards and endeavouring to adapt the major-domo model after years of advisers focusing on specialisms?

But the main argument in favour of the high-performing advisory team must be presented from the perspective of family businesses, rather than whether it is convenient for advisers. Surely it is reasonable for family businesses to be able to invest their trust in a team of specialists who can show the family how they will collaborate and who can each contribute expertise in service of whatever version of success the family is striving to achieve?

This special report has four overall aims:

- Unpack the notion of trust to identify the effect of different elements on the relationship between a family business and its advisers;
- Debunk the view that the trusted adviser to a family business is an individual specialist who possesses some soft skills and can confidently espouse so-called 'best practices';
- Look at how different answers to the deceptively simple question, "Who do you trust?" affect the relationships between a family business and their advisers; and
- Suggest how the idea of a trusted team of advisers for a family business could work in practice, including having a new type of family business advisers' constitution.

We need to talk about specialists

A family whose lives are connected through a business occasionally need help from various specialist advisers, including in the fields of law, finance, tax, accounting, banking, insurance, employment, human resources, business strategy, IT and so on. Each adviser will be expected to be a trusted repository of specialist know-how and skills that the family and its business need in order to deal with situations that are too complex to cope with on their own.

There are good reasons why specialisation is now the dominant business model among advisers:

- The increasing array of laws and regulations that affect a family and its business mean that one adviser cannot know everything.
- The constant reiteration that change always quickens its pace represents a business opportunity for advisers who specialise in understanding these changes and can communicate this know-how to family business clients.
- It reflects a desire among advisers to provide a better-quality service and reduce the risk of family businesses receiving incorrect advice.
- Like any division of labour, specialisms are more profitable for advisers – at least for as long as a specialism remains special and does not become a commodity.

With all these strengths, what could possibly be the problem with this advisory model? The answer must be presented from the perspective of a family business and not from that of an adviser, because advisers who devote their careers to a specialism are unlikely to see the source of their professional identity, status and wealth as a problem. The following account of one family business's experience is intended to be whimsical, but it also contains some challenging truths.

1. The sedative effect of specialist advice

The clients – husband and wife co-preneurs who founded a successful business – seek help from an adviser called Mr Smith. They do not have specific instructions that require immediate action; their motivation for arranging to meet is a growing concern that time is marching on and there has been little discussion about how and when they will retire and whether any of their children, the next generation, want either to take over managing the family business or to inherit a share of ownership.

There are four in the next generation, all of adult age, well-educated and quite sensible. The eldest currently works in the business, although his parents admit that he is not the most talented of their offspring. The other siblings have pursued different careers and lifestyles and resisted their parents' encouragement to consider a career in the family business – mostly with good humour, but not without the occasional argument.

The clients are worried about treating the family fairly because most of their wealth is tied up in the business. At the same time, as owners and directors, they want to be fair and considerate to the business and all its stakeholders, including employees, customers and suppliers. They are also sensitive about the family's reputation being closely connected with the business, especially since the family surname is used as the company's well-known brand.

In this type of meeting, clients often reveal information and float ideas for the future in an understated, even haphazard, fashion – which is understandable, because they have many things to worry about. The conversation ranges freely across their version of retirement (which does not sound much like retirement to Mr Smith) and on to management succession, which is linked to who can become an owner; which leads to a brief discussion about each of the next generation before the topic changes to personal financial planning and pensions for the founders. The clients admit that one of the reasons for delaying discussions about the future is that they do not know what they will do if they retire and they like the status that comes with being well known in their industry. The conversation then swings back to personal financial planning because the clients are not sure that they can afford to retire if this means giving up their current income from the business.

If Mr Smith feels slightly overwhelmed and uncertain about how to address the range of issues that the clients are unloading, and others that he might guess at, he may endeavour to use his specialist knowledge to filter this information and identify where he can help. This means help in areas where his technical specialism is relevant. While this is understandable, it does not mean that it is always helpful. Although Mr Smith, with relative ease, can bring some sense of order to what he feels is a chaotic discussion by interpreting what needs to be done through the lens of his specialism, from the clients' perspective, the world looks a lot less focused.

They are unlikely to understand the technical matters that they did not know about before Mr Smith introduced them to the conversation. In any case, they feel that these do not entirely address all the doubts and fears about the future that prompted them to arrange a meeting in the first place and, regrettably, Mr Smith uses quite a lot of technical jargon.

Mr Smith, however, believes that displaying an ability to provide answers quickly will impress the clients, which can be achieved by him focusing the conversation on what he knows. It must also be acknowledged that

"Each adviser will be expected to be a trusted repository of specialist know-how and skills that the family and its business need in order to deal with situations that are too complex to cope with on their own."

"Advice from different specialists recommending different solutions and sometimes even disagreeing over what is the best technical approach could have an unintended sedative effect on family businesses."

if Mr Smith either charges for his services based on some measure of time or has a product to sell, there is an organisational imperative forcing him – or, if that is too strong, at least encouraging him – to do something that will be chargeable to the clients, rather than just listening to them unloading their views about the many challenges that come with being a family in business together.

The effect of Mr Smith hastening the discussions to a conclusion that represents value for him can be compared to jumping on a train (represented by the clients) that is gathering speed (their anxieties about the future) and then trying to help by shovelling in more coal to make the train reach a destination faster. If the destination reached under Mr Smith's specialist direction is called 'tax plan' or 'retirement funding package' or 'life insurance' or 'will' or 'trust' or 'sale mandate' or 'shareholders' agreement', the clients might be wondering, "How did we end up here when we were trying to work out how to divide ownership among all the kids and who to appoint as the next leader of our business?"

The swiftness with which Mr Smith responds to the clients' vague enquiries about the future leaves them slightly more anxious than when they started out that morning. After recuperating over lunch, the clients meet Mrs Brown, who comes from a different specialist background; but sadly the morning's experiences are largely repeated. Brown focuses on other technical matters that are within her area of specialism. She tries to explain these to the clients before concluding, with the intention of being helpful, "You don't really need to know all this stuff – that's what I'm here for."

This satisfies Brown's urge to display her specialist prowess, although it simultaneously adds to the clients' confusion and as a result their anxiety about the future is now turning into a sense of dread. Brown signs off with the cheery suggestion that she will prepare a comprehensive report for the clients and they can get back in touch after they have read it and decided what to do.

After a busy day, the founders of this successful family business feel that they have more problems of a technical nature than they knew about when setting out that morning in the hope of finding ideas about the way forward for the family and the business. While all the advice was well intentioned and, they assume, technically accurate, the clients are unsure whether they are any closer to answering the questions that really concern them – questions such as, "Do the next generation want to take over the family business or become owners, given that two of them do not get on?" It occurs to them that this snippet of information about family relationship difficulties never entered the discussions; but then again, no one asked, and as parents the clients did not want to admit to these family difficulties – who would?

Advice from different specialists recommending different solutions and sometimes even disagreeing over what is the best technical approach could have an unintended sedative effect on family businesses.[1] After the sedative wears off, they could be excused for deciding to avoid the pain of trying to plan for the future by adopting that most popular of succession planning options: do nothing and hope for the best.

The experts featured in this scenario, and their supporters, might suggest that the family clearly needs help from yet another specialist. Perhaps one of the growing number of family business consultants who specialise in grappling with the economic and emotional forces at play during an inter-generational transition could help the family to discover who among the next generation want to become owners and whether any of them is willing and able to take on a leadership role. After these issues have been resolved, the other specialists can re-enter the fray and help the family to implement the agreed outcome by applying their technical know-how in relation to tax, law, finance, employment, personal financial planning and so on.

1 Thanks to my colleague and friend Amy Renkert-Thomas for lending me this phrase.

The clients, however, could be excused for worrying about whether advice from such a gaggle of different specialists will inevitably and spontaneously meld into a coherent plan for the family and the business. Is there a risk, they wonder, of the specialists working in isolation of each other and the family ending up with fragments of advice that they are then somehow meant to fit together? Also, they are concerned that the advisers might compete with each other in the hope of securing more work from the family business at the expense of another adviser.

The answer to all these questions is, of course, that the clients need another specialist – a project manager this time, who organises all the other advisers and tempers their competitive instincts. Some families would scoff at this suggestion, purely on the basis that this is really one adviser too many for anyone to contemplate. Others would reject it because they prefer to have control over their advisers and would find the idea of delegating this responsibility to another adviser outside the family to be distinctly odd. These families would tend to agree with the economist Adam Smith that "people of the same trade seldom meet together, even for merriment and diversion, but the conversation ends in a conspiracy against the public, or in some contrivance to raise prices". They would, therefore, prefer a family member to be in charge of coordinating a series of strictly bilateral relationships with all the

"Many specialists and business families would now be sceptical about whether an individual adviser could advise a family and its business ambidextrously in respect of all their needs to a uniformly high standard of professionalism."

different specialist advisers, who would then lack any opportunity to conspire against the family's interests.

However, there will be families which feel that they do not have the necessary skills to coordinate the wide variety of advice being offered to them and their business. Many will simply prefer to pay someone to do this for them and focus their time on more gainful or pleasurable pursuits, such as running the business or planning what to do in retirement. If the family prefers not to hire a specialist project manager to carry out this coordinating role, then maybe it can assign the task to an existing adviser.

2. The ambidextrous, T-shaped gatekeeper

The ambidextrous adviser could be described as one who can understand what is needed by the family and the business and advise accordingly. This seems to be the modern equivalent of the general practitioner, who sometimes was also referred to as the *homme d'affaires, consigliere* or major-domo. But in the current era, when everyone is a specialist for good reasons, the general practitioner has become largely extinct as a species. Many specialists and business families would now be sceptical about whether an individual adviser could advise a family and its business ambidextrously in respect of all their needs to a uniformly high standard of professionalism.

The riposte to this is that the modern ambidextrous adviser is neither the contemporary equivalent of a general practitioner nor expected to advise the family and its business on all matters. Instead, this adviser will combine a deep specialism in one area of what the family business needs with an ability to understand and apply knowledge from other areas and to coordinate the other advisers on behalf of the client. Another description for this type of adviser is 'T-shaped' – combining a specialism, whose depth is represented by the vertical bar on the T, with the ability to apply knowledge from other areas of expertise and work with other experts, this being the horizontal bar.

Others have compared the role of coordinating adviser as being analogous to a quarterback who leads the team or a conductor who directs an ensemble to perform to the best of their abilities. This analogy is valid if it refers to an important role in a well-functioning team, or ensemble, of advisers who serve a family business; but it is flawed if it refers to a single member of a multi-specialist team.

For example, if a family business is acquiring another business, the adviser who specialises in such work will lead the team and, in the role of quarterback or conductor, will call on other advisers when their skills are needed – for example, in relation to tax, property, pensions, employment and so on. But when the task is to create a tax plan or buy a property or invest money, the identity of the quarterback or conductor must change to another adviser with the relevant specialism, who decides how and when to instruct other advisers whose expertise is needed to complete the task at hand.

This leads to the rather obvious conclusion that there cannot be a single trusted adviser to a family business; what is needed is a team of specialists who can be trusted in their own areas of expertise, are willing to collaborate and, when necessary, can each also perform the role of quarterback or conductor to a high standard. Every adviser must be willing and able to be a good team player and to take direction from whoever assumes leadership of the team from time to time. However, this idea of the trusted team of advisers contradicts the more popular view that every family business needs one T-shaped or ambidextrous adviser who is more trusted than the others and who is permanently the go-to person for the family and the other advisers.

The idea of the single trusted adviser appeals to advisers who would like to play a more strategic role in relation to a family business client, instead of being limited to operating permanently in their specialist silos. The trusted role at the centre of the family business could also be profitable for the adviser where work for the family and its business can be referred to other specialists in the same organisation as the trusted adviser. There is nothing wrong with these ambitions, from the perspective of the adviser who has a business to run; but there is a risk that cross-selling to a family and its business in this way may be deemed untrustworthy behaviour by clients who feel that advisers should never place their own self-interest before the interests of the client.

Families might also be a little worried when they come across another term that is used as a synonym for 'trusted adviser': the 'gatekeeper'. The gatekeeper's status is reflected in how other advisers and family members must pass through the gatekeeper in order to meet each other. The clue to the difficulty is in the name and the risk of the gatekeeper misusing this power to keep advisers and the family apart – especially any advisers who might benefit the family, but threaten the gatekeeper's favoured position. The gatekeeper, in other words, may succumb to the temptation to keep the family business captive, which is unlikely to be considered to be in the best interests of a family and its business by any standards, least of all the standards of utmost good faith inherent in a trusted relationship.

3. Moving forwards by looking backwards

The idea of the single most trusted adviser is an effort by advisers to move beyond the self-imposed limitations caused by their narrow technical specialisms by looking backwards – nostalgically, perhaps – to an earlier age of general practice. This mind set dooms specialists to competing for a rather confused role that could be described as an ambidextrous, T-shaped conductor with the talent to be a quarterback gatekeeper. It is doubtful that there are many advisers with this range of skills and attributes; or even that there are many willing candidates when the role is described this way. Indeed, how many family businesses want this type of so-called 'trusted adviser'?

Where does this leave the notion of a trusted adviser in the era of specialisms? As has already been suggested, family businesses need advice from a team of specialists who can be trusted to deliver in their respective areas of expertise and who have the skills to lead the advisory team when necessary. As a team, the advisers will help the family to make decisions about the future and then implement these wishes without any of them being distracted by competing with others for the favoured status of most trusted adviser overall.

A key strategic question is whether specialists want to be part of this type of high-performing team. Advisers who read to the end of this special report will hopefully gain some ideas about the opportunities of creating this type of team; but at this stage, it is worth mentioning potential threats to the specialist business model that may affect the willingness of advisers to meet the challenges that this will involve.

"There cannot be a single trusted adviser to a family business. What is needed is a team of specialists who can be trusted in their own areas of expertise."

In the past, advisers' control or power over knowledge was bolstered by restrictive practices in professions that made it difficult for anyone else – including family businesses – to access, understand and use this knowledge. Advisers also enjoyed elevated social status, which was supported by a deferential attitude towards professionals that was based on more rigid social hierarchies than those which exist now in many societies.

Whether professional advisers still enjoy some level of enhanced status and respect is debatable, but there is no doubt that restrictive practices in many professions are being dismantled in the related causes of consumerism and opening up professions to greater competition and new business models. While these developments are putting many advisers under increased pressure, the vibrancy of the specialist model is also coming under threat from the practices of specialists themselves.

For reasons of economic self-interest, advisers willingly conspire against perpetuating the competitive advantages that a specialism confers. They commoditise their specialisms so that work can be delegated and the specialist's output – or productivity or utilisation – can be increased or leveraged. This delegation generates more fees for specialists and helps to develop new ones, while also in theory providing more clients with access to specialisms at a reasonable cost.

Paradoxically, over time, this can result in specialists undermining their specialism. Breaking a specialism down into delegable tasks carries the risk of deskilling the specialism and eventually what was once special ends up being not so special anymore. The business model that drives a better financial return from specialisation tends to result in the specialism losing its scarcity value and becoming a commodity.

Loosening advisers' control over specialist knowledge, however, is being driven by forces that are far more potent than advisers trying to increase near-term profits by delegating some work. The process of commoditisation is being accelerated by increasing reliance on organisations that provide automated knowledge services and it probably will not be long until some current specialisms become extinct, in a way that is similar to how specialisms led to the downfall of general practitioners.

The future of advising family businesses is unlikely to involve attempting to resurrect the general practitioner model as some form of solo, ambidextrous or T-shaped adviser. Instead, it involves specialist advisers figuring out how to collaborate in an inter-disciplinary team to serve the interests of a family and its business.

Do not trust best practice

The phrases 'trusted adviser' and 'best practice' are often found in close proximity, as though one of the attributes of a trusted adviser is the ability to identify the best practices for organising the affairs of a family and its business. Proponents of a best practice approach are obviously undeterred by another phrase, 'every family is different', which on the face of it hints that what might be best for one family business will not suit another. Best practice, in contrast, promotes the belief that all family businesses are similar in sufficient ways for some practices to be denoted as being universally, or simply, the best. This approach, however, does not deliver what it promises and trying to fit family businesses to the notion of best practice in fact threatens to harm those whom it is supposed to help.

1. What is best, and worst?
A simple example helps to illustrate a point.

Every family business at the sibling stage faces the challenge of family members having to form an effective ownership and management team while addressing the diverse and possibly competing interests in a growing family. The best practice recommendations for this family business would include the following:

"Proponents of a best practice approach are undeterred by the phrase, 'every family is different', which hints that what might be best for one family business will not suit another."

- Agree which sibling will be in overall charge of the business to avoid either a leadership struggle or a vacuum.
- Establish formal structures such as a board of directors and a family council to ensure that business and family matters can be addressed separately.
- Create an employment policy to govern how family members get jobs in the business so that the respective needs of the business and the family are well balanced.

These recommendations combine the practical experiences of some sibling partnerships with the opinions of various practitioners and researchers. This is a potent combination and is certainly of interest to families which are keen to know how others have resolved similar dilemmas; but does it all deserve to be called best practice?

There are cases of siblings who want to stay in business, but are uncomfortable about working closely together. They fear that having to decide who has the overall leadership role will create conflict and they shy away from meeting in the formal settings of either a boardroom or a family council because these meetings could be excruciating and risk triggering arguments. Instead, they organise the business so that each sibling can control a part of it separately from the others.

The siblings in effect adapt to the pressures of collective ownership and control by creating operational silos in their business, which keep them apart. These may be divisions in the same business – for example, one sibling may be in charge of manufacturing, while another controls sales and a third manages finance. The silo arrangement could be constituted in separate subsidiaries within a corporate group or as separate companies in different locations, but the overall effect is the same. Each family member can operate his or her silo with significant autonomy, safe in the knowledge that no one else will interfere. It may even be accepted that this extends to each sibling having authority to employ his or her children in the relevant silo, instead of having a formal policy for employing the next generation that applies across the business.

This family will have no one in overall charge, will prefer to avoid board meetings and will regard the idea of the family meeting in the formal setting of a family council as distinctly odd. It will also have solved the delicate issue of how family members can become employed in the business. If these arrangements work well, should they be promoted as an example of best practice? This, of course, would be ludicrous, because they will not suit every family; but the same goes for so-called 'best practices', which clearly do not suit this family. Families that use the silo approach to run a successful business certainly do not deserve to be accused of adopting worst practices, but this must be the corollary of routinely blessing the alternatives as being the best.

2. The best practice fallacy

There is a notable tendency among best practice devotees to apply ideas from other disciplines to family businesses. This is probably partly due to family business being an emerging field of practice, which means it is easier for advisers to enter the market by promoting their existing services as an example of best practice rather than patiently building a new body of knowledge and experience.

For example, people who are familiar with conventional corporate governance for companies whose shares are publicly traded are often keen to promote this as being the best practice model for governance of larger, privately owned family businesses. The assumption is that the way to improve corporate governance in a family business is to eradicate the dysfunctional practices that can be exposed by benchmarking what the family business does against the codes and guidelines that apply to a listed company.

This is very worrying, because corporate governance for listed companies is based on assumptions that do not fit the needs and expectations of every family business, as summarised in Table 1.

Table 1. UK corporate governance compared to family businesses

UK listed public companies	Family businesses
Publicly owned	Mainly private companies
Dispersed ownership	Concentrated family ownership
Predominant role of financial institutions	Predominant role of an owning family
Shareholder value is paramount	Family seeks a mixture of returns on investment, and not all of them are entirely economic
Short-term investor commitment	Long-term family commitment
Short-term performance measurement	Long-term investment horizon
High financial leverage and creative accounting	Low financial leverage and cautious accounting

These are major differences, but there is an even more fundamental mismatch to worry about. In broad terms, the Anglo-American model of corporate governance is based on the principal-agent problem: how do you motivate one party (a director) to act on behalf of others (the shareholders) when it is assumed that the director will act in his or her own self-interest and thus against the interests of the shareholders?

This problem of the director being the agent of the shareholder means that corporate governance for listed companies is based on the owners' distrust of management. Rules in the form of codes and guidelines and formal mechanisms and enforcement are needed to mitigate the type of opportunistic management behaviour that might result in reduced shareholder returns. Hence, for example, share options are used to align the interests of management with those of the shareholders. The argument in favour of such incentives is that management with equity are more likely to act in the interests of the shareholders, since this also serves the managers' interests.

Shareholders and directors in some family businesses may feel that they have similar problems in trusting each other and find listed company corporate governance to be a good fit for their needs. On the other hand, such an approach to governance is the opposite to what many family businesses prefer. These families want governance structures and practices that reflect relationships of loyalty and trust, rather than being based on distrust. They might reasonably argue that their preferred approach to governance will encourage teamwork, foster long-term commitment among owners and avoid unnecessary bureaucracy, management by rulebook and short-term performance measurement. These advantages are surely worth pursuing; in which case the levers and controls of conventional corporate governance are not of much use, let alone being an example of so-called 'best practice'.

Claiming that the best practice for privately owned family businesses should be based on corporate governance for public companies can justifiably be denigrated as a form of corporatist imperialism – an attempt to extend the power and influence of a supposedly supreme form of corporate governance to subordinate types of business. It can also be ridiculed as being no more sensible as saying, "This drug works for species A, so it must work for species B, even though they are very different in many ways."

The broader fallacy that lies at the heart of best practice claims is that it judges a family business against a set of standards or norms that lie outside the family which owns that business. It is risky and in many cases plain wrong to suggest that a practice or structure that works effectively either in another type of business or even for another family business ought to work for every family business; but this is exactly what the best practice approach does.

3. The risk of doing damage

The best practice approach could indeed damage the family businesses that it is supposedly trying to help. The way that a family organises its personal affairs and governs its business will always reflect its values, culture and relationships. The silo version of governance mentioned earlier illustrates the point. It works by creating distance between siblings who have difficulty communicating with each other. The silos keep direct communication to a minimum and whenever decisions need collaboration, this can be done as quickly as possible in meetings that are as short as possible. Between meetings, messages may be passed through deputies who do not suffer the same anxiety as the siblings about getting together.

The advice that this group of siblings ought to hold more regular board meetings because this is considered to be best practice is useless, for the obvious reason that they prefer to avoid this type of interaction. If they held regular board meetings, it is likely that the amount of time and energy that would be invested (the siblings might prefer to say 'wasted') in doing so could be damaging. As long as business and family life are successful for the siblings and their business, what is wrong with their way of doing things?

The family would likely describe the way it organises its business as "How we do things around here". Importantly, this represents the family's version of normal. In this context, 'normal' means how an overall balance is achieved among the competing interests in the family and in the business. When the family and business are in balance, life feels good, and the family would say that it has a functional way of running the business that is normal for that family no matter how odd it appears to outsiders, including advisers.

The impact of recommending that this family business change what it does and adopt so-called 'best practices' could be the opposite of what is intended. The apparently functional best practice, such as holding board meetings, could in fact be completely dysfunctional for the family when compared to its own version of normal. While the family can cope with its version of the apparently dysfunctional, it may be unable to adapt to what an outside adviser would consider to be normal or best practice because this would be potentially dysfunctional for the family.

There is a danger of knocking a family business completely off balance if all that is done is to try to make the supposedly dysfunctional more functional by using a version of normal that sits outside that family business. Referring to these external standards as best practices seems more likely to make the family feel worse about how its business is organised and run, which is downright odd if what the family is doing works. How will a family ever trust an adviser who threatens it with best practice in this way?

4. Conventional wisdom

The counterargument, however, might be that the above is a narrow-minded, literal interpretation of best practice. Best practice is meant to be more like the conventional wisdom described by economist John Kenneth Galbraith in his book *The Affluent Society*:[2] "It will be convenient to have a name for the ideas which are esteemed at any time for their acceptability, and it should be a term that emphasises this predictability. I shall refer to these ideas henceforth as the conventional wisdom."

Instead of the view that there is one best practice in every area of family business life, the conventional wisdom provides business families with ideas that are currently esteemed as being the most

2 John Kenneth Galbraith, *The Affluent Society* (Boston, Mass: Houghton Mifflin 1958).

"Conventional wisdom makes vigorous advocacy of originality a substitute for originality itself."

John Kenneth Galbraith

acceptable. Since family business is a relatively new field of knowledge and practice, this wisdom comprises results from academic research, examples of how other families have created successful businesses and what can be learned from unrelated types of enterprise, such as public listed companies.

Galbraith's explanation of the conventional wisdom continues as follows:

> *Numerous factors contribute to the acceptability of ideas. To a very large extent, of course, we associate truth with convenience – with what most closely accords with self-interest and individual well-being or promises best to avoid awkward effort or unwelcome dislocation of life. ... But perhaps most important of all, people approve most of what they best understand. ... Therefore we adhere, as though to a raft, to those ideas which represent our understanding. This is a prime manifestation of vested interest. For a vested interest in understanding is more preciously guarded than any other treasure. It is why men react, not infrequently with something akin to religious passion, to the defence of what they have so laboriously learned. Familiarity may breed contempt in some areas of human behaviour, but in the field of social ideas it is the touchstone of acceptability.*

"While it is useful for families to know how others govern their business or organise their family affairs, each of them is likely to prefer to do things differently."

In place of "the field of social ideas", one could insert "the professions which advise family businesses". This alerts us to the need to identify the manifestation of a vested interest, which is the correlation between best practice recommendations – or the conventional wisdom – and the services offered by its proponents. Advisers with deep specialisms built on hard-won knowledge and experience that they need to sell in order to earn income understandably can succumb to the temptation of claiming that whatever they advise is an example of best practice or conventional wisdom. That vested interest might be concealed by some good marketing, but it is still a vested interest.

Galbraith is pessimistic about the conventional wisdom ever changing from within because of the self-interest of its supporters. He also warns that new ideas tend to be repelled by the conventional wisdom because they are perceived as a threat and "the conventional wisdom makes vigorous advocacy of originality a substitute for originality itself".

However, while original ideas may pose a repellable threat to the conventional wisdom, the real enemy of convention is what Galbraith describes as "the march of events". As we learn more about how complex family businesses function, we learn about the inadequacy of advice based on either best practice or the conventional wisdom. We develop a humble awareness that family businesses thrive on their own resources without knowing what others call best practice or conventional wisdom. This provides a clue to an advisory approach to serving family businesses that is centred on their experience and is therefore more likely to gain their trust. An initial brief description may help families and advisers to march together in the same general direction and find something of value in the remainder of this special report.

5. An alternative approach

The first step is to recognise that a family's version of what is best practice is likely to be based on "This works fine for us", rather than "This is what someone else thinks is best for us".

For example, instead of being advised to change from the silo arrangement described earlier because it is supposedly dysfunctional, a business family would benefit from advisers who can understand and respect that this is how the family prefers to organise and run its business. When the family and adviser both understand this current reality as the norm, they can explore whether it is feasible for the family's future in business together.

Continuing the silo version of governance into the next generation could involve one child in each branch taking over from the parent.

This might involve some difficult discussions in each branch about who should be the successor and about the abilities of each branch's candidate; but these are discussions worth having, rather than what has worked for the family being needlessly swept aside.

This is a client-centric approach, in which advisers seek to stand in the shoes of the family business and comprehend the way that it understands and gives meaning to its world. Of course, it is impossible for an adviser to enter the family's world completely; but helping to improve the situation as understood and defined by the family, based on its culture, values and traditions, is still preferable to advising the family and its business to do things that are based on practices that are external to its reality and experiences.

The tests that matter for every family business are not whether it is perfect when measured by an outside standard that an adviser – often for reasons of self-interest – decrees is best practice or conventional wisdom. The relevant standards are more likely to be the following:

- Does the family's existing way of organising its affairs and governing its business help it to achieve – and not hinder it from achieving – its version of success?
- Can it be adapted in a way that is acceptable to the family in order to remain functional in the future?

Sweeping statements of best practice and conventional wisdom deserve to be met with a sweeping response. They are often excessive generalisations from selected examples leading to complex family businesses being reduced to facile slogans that are falsely presented as universal laws. While it is useful for families to know how others govern their business or organise their family affairs, each of them is likely to prefer to do things differently.

The best help that a business family can get is probably from advisers who can be trusted partly because they have no best practices to sell.

Soft skills are not enough

It is often suggested that the trusted adviser to a family business is one who possesses soft skills. This refers to an indistinct cluster of personal characteristics around listening and communication that enable the adviser to build personal relationships. These skills are particularly useful when the adviser encounters the emotional issues, or so-called 'soft stuff', that every family business must deal with at some time and are distinct from the adviser's specialism or technical know-how, which represents the 'hard stuff'.

This is, of course, an adviser-centric view of the world. Family businesses would reasonably argue that the nomenclature should be reversed, because the 'soft stuff' is in fact the 'hard stuff'. There is no doubt that an adviser who engages with the emotional dimension of key decisions that every family business must make will have an advantage over those who fail or refuse to do so, but more elements go into establishing a trusted relationship between a family business and its advisers than just combining an adviser's specialism with some so-called 'soft skills'. First, however, a bit more about soft skills and the role of emotional intelligence (EI) in advising family businesses.

1. Emotional intelligence

Enterprising families often seek advice when emotions resulting from anxiety about a situation or the future in general cannot be contained and so become sufficient to prompt action:

- There is often fear that the absence of a workable plan for the transition of ownership and leadership in the family business will lead to loss of money, status and reputation and threaten family relationships.
- Equally, there could be fear that starting to discuss such a plan will itself cause conflict.
- The trigger for seeking advice could be a family or business crisis, entailing feelings of grief, sadness and maybe even symptoms of depression.
- People may feel vulnerable, angry and frustrated for a number of reasons, including the effect that the business is having on family relationships or the way family issues are playing out in the business.

Fear. Loss. Conflict. Grief. Sadness. Depression. Anger. Frustration. Every adviser to a family business will at some stage encounter these emotions – and, of course, more positive emotions such as hope, love, and possibly irrational exuberance about the business's future prospects. Since it is impossible to separate emotion from business – although some advisers cling to this delusion – EI is a characteristic that business families may value in their trusted advisers.

"Enterprising families often seek advice when emotions resulting from anxiety about a situation or the future in general cannot be contained."

Some believe that EI is a trait; others argue that it can be learned. Either way, given that every family business is a circuit board of anxiety-inducing relationships and events that are refracted through emotions, the savvy and trusted adviser to a family business will want to know how to read emotions. This knowledge will also help the adviser to understand the impact that the client's emotional reactions have on the adviser.

In the absence of some EI, there is a risk of the adviser remaining detached from these emotions or seeking to get a grip on matters by using other coping mechanisms, such as his or her technical specialism. This distancing from the emotions at play in every family business might be justified as being necessary to enable the adviser to remain objective and to focus on the so-called 'hard stuff' – a stance that is reinforced by emphasising the need for the adviser to be rational and apply some clear, hard-headed thinking. But in truth, this attitude is likely to be about the adviser's inability or lack of training when it comes to participating in emotionally charged discussions with family businesses.

EI is a demanding standard to expect of trusted advisers to family businesses. But EI or soft skills, plus a specialism, overlook other powerful elements that go into developing a trusting relationship between a family business and its advisers. These are:

- the reality of economic necessity;
- the power relationship between the adviser and the family business;
- the competence of the parties;
- the impact of external regulation; and
- the way that trusting relationships are affected by organisations and their marketing.

2. Economic necessity

I recently entrusted my life to complete strangers, having beforehand given some personal financial data to another stranger for mere pleasure. The idea of being generally trusting of strangers to this extent may be scoffed at, but not if the sentence is rewritten.

I recently boarded an aircraft having beforehand used my credit card to pay for a meal. I shall never have a relationship with the pilot or any of the aircraft crew, or with the restaurant staff, but I decided to trust them anyway.

Trust, of course, is an economic lubricant that is used out of necessity. It is immensely powerful given that we continue to extend trust to those who have proved themselves to be untrustworthy. For example, even if the airline loses my luggage or the restaurant has had some previous health and safety issues, I may still in future choose to fly with the same airline and eat before boarding rather than trust the in-flight catering in economy class.

As another example, we still work with and to some extent trust financial institutions even though we have come to expect at any moment another disclosure involving the loss of personal data, market rigging or mis-selling. The economic role of trust is, therefore, not entirely rational: if I have evidence of untrustworthiness, I should be wary of investing my trust; but I need to do this in order for life to function, so necessity overcomes rationality.

Every family business will use an adviser, to some extent, because it needs to; and some families probably consider their advisers to be the ultimate distress purchase, saying things such as, "We only use you because we have to." They will trust the adviser who completes a task on time and on budget, and have little interest in developing a personal relationship with – or even liking – the adviser.

The adviser may harbour similar feelings. Clients are awkward people who complicate matters by sometimes not following the adviser's sage advice and they make excessive demands on the adviser's time while paying as little as can be negotiated for this service. The adviser, in more candid moments, might admit that clients are to be tolerated because the adviser needs to earn a living.

This could be the perfect trusted relationship between a family business and adviser – one in which trust is based on economic necessity and mutual tolerance, and is not burdened with expectations that it should involve any more by way of a relationship than what is needed to get a job done.

3. Competency and the effect of regulation

How much does trust in competence matter? To go back up in the air, flying involves investing trust in the airline to train and monitor the staff to whom I have entrusted my life. While cruising at 36,000 feet, I might wonder whether trustworthiness is a competency that was measured when recruiting staff and whether this was reviewed during their most recent appraisals. However, I do not have the means to carry out personal checks on every pilot so – again, partly out of economic necessity – I assume that incompetents have been weeded out. If experience proves this to be completely wrong, I will certainly choose to use another airline, if I survive the experience.

Back on the ground, I have broadly the same approach to my dentist, doctor, car mechanic and electrician, all of whom I have to trust because I need their help and I do not understand what they do. A family business, however, does not need to take the competency of its advisers entirely for granted in this way. It will often check the adviser's credentials, sometimes privately or more obviously by requesting references or holding a beauty parade. This all helps, but only goes so far. A family will struggle to decide whether one specialist is more competent or knowledgeable than another. If a family could make such an informed judgement about specialisms, then it would probably be expert enough not to need an expert. This means that at some level, a family business must trust the competence of an adviser and then update and adjust its beliefs in line with evidence of performance.

But this leaves unanswered the question: how much does trust in competence matter? Some argue that on most occasions it is taken for granted, such as in the example of the pilot, and that the added value for both adviser and family lies in developing a personal relationship of some sort. The adviser will be expected to perform well, but – so the argument goes – a business family will expect more from the adviser than just a good track record of competent performance. The family and the adviser might agree that personal chemistry is vital, or might feel more comfortable transacting if they share some other social connections.

The retort to this is that competence matters above all else and far more than any notions of either the adviser or the family business having what might be described as a 'good bedside manner'. Everyone's trust in a pilot is to take off and land the aircraft safely, preferably on schedule, and these competencies matter far more than whether we happen to like the pilot as a person. The same could be said for any service provider – be that a dentist, doctor, accountant, lawyer or financial adviser.

The outcome of this debate will depend on the respective personal biases of a family business and advisers, but it is worth an adviser considering whether it is wise investing a lot of time and money trying to build personal relationships with a family that rates competency more highly than appealing personal characteristics.

Advisers are also, of course, concerned about the competency of their clients. They carry out formal checks to ensure that the client is not a criminal or a credit risk. In this regard, regulations have almost entirely replaced making judgements based on a personal connection between the family and the adviser, or even the reliability of a mutual contact who introduced the family and adviser to each other. It is ironic that such external regulation of professions, which is intended to benefit advisers and clients, has probably contributed to a diminution in trust between them. Professional standards, codes of ethics, practice

"Being worthy of trust imposes constant demands in trying situations and trust in an organisation or an individual can be betrayed by ineptitude or corruption."

regulations and so forth in some measure aim to control any temptation among advisers to use their power and technical competence to gain an unfair advantage over the family business. This regulatory intervention is laudable, but also reflects a lack of willingness to assume that advisers can be trusted to act benevolently in clients' best interests. Efforts to promote the interests of clients through increased regulation of advisers have contributed to an atmosphere of distrust and the view that advisers are not to be trusted entirely to play fair or to regulate themselves.

4. Trust in organisations

Which comes first for a family business: trust in an individual adviser or trust in the organisation that he or she represents?

Some argue that trust in organisations is built on or extends from the family trusting individual advisers and so the individual relationship always comes first. The contrary argument is that a family business wants advisers who can serve it in the longer term, even into succeeding generations; so first and foremost, it invests trust in an organisation to train advisers now and in the future.

Being worthy of trust imposes constant demands in trying situations and trust in an organisation or an individual can be betrayed by ineptitude or corruption. During the 2008 financial crisis, for example, the need to support family businesses during difficult times came up against the need for some advisory organisations to repair their balance sheets and generate short-term returns. The perception is that, when tested, some advisers acted in their self-interest and this resulted in a loss of trust among the family businesses they served. But did this also taint the personal relationships between families and the individual advisers who worked for those organisations?

In some cases the individual advisers no doubt took the brunt of their organisations' failings and relationships were harmed. In others, the strength of a personal relationship between the adviser and the family business rescued the organisation from losing a connection due to its corporate misdeeds. The same dynamic, of course, can work in reverse and there will be times when the possibly dire consequences of inept performance by an individual adviser will be rescued by the reputation of the organisation and its ability to field a suitable substitute.

Family businesses invest trust in both organisations and individual advisers to varying extents and this argument cannot be settled one way or the other. While trust in an individual adviser will be based mainly on the direct personal experience of those in the family business, the organisational reputation will have something to do with marketing.

5. Marketing trust

Trust is often represented by a brand image and, therefore, it is interesting to reflect on how organisations market their trustworthiness to family businesses.

It is popular to focus on the problems facing family businesses. The marketing message is that if you are in pain or feel ill, the adviser has specialist skills and can provide the necessary cure. And if you do not feel ill right now, it is a good time to take preventative action because otherwise you are bound to suffer in future.

This worrying message is often emphasised by stressing the risk of family businesses never surviving beyond three generations. This presses on a deeply embedded social narrative that is conveyed through clichés such as 'clogs to clogs' or 'shirtsleeves to shirtsleeves' in three generations. This denouement is presented as an inevitable tragedy that awaits every family business other than those which accept the help of skilled advisers.

How encouraging is this as a way for an organisation to build trust? It seems to be based on the view that fear sells. It pathologises the family business: first, diagnose an illness or the threat thereof and then, after the fear has been pumped up, offer a cure or preventative measures. While some may respond positively to being told they are ill or in danger of becoming so, an equally likely response is that the family business ignores the threatening message in preference to getting on with enjoying life – which, on reflection, is relatively good and certainly not anywhere near as bad as the miserable state outlined by advisers.

This response may be based on a family's belief that it will not suffer the terrible problems that affect other family businesses. Whether this is viewed as realistic or naively optimistic is a matter of opinion, affected by temperament and perspective. Many family businesses have an optimistic outlook that enables them to take entrepreneurial risks that others, including advisers, would find intolerable. Advisers, one could argue, are paid to be professionally pessimistic and anticipate undesirable outcomes.

The fear style of marketing also assumes that a family business is willing to entrust its adviser with power to diagnose a problem and that the family or business will then take whatever medicine is prescribed. That requires a lot of trust on the part of the family – which is often a mistaken assumption, because when facing critical decisions about the future of the family and its business, a family often wants to have significant control over decision making. In making the big decisions, the family business client will trust its own judgements and will not always buy into the notion that the adviser knows best.

"An alternative approach to marketing a trusting relationship is for advisers to recognise that a thriving family business has succeeded without much guidance from advisers."

If the patient (sorry, family business) refuses to take the medicine or other action to avoid a prescription becoming necessary, the temptation among advisers might be to blame the family business. However, the adviser might also want to consider other ways of gaining trust rather than continuing to threaten a family business with the dire consequences of inaction.

Fear sells, but so does hope. An alternative approach to marketing a trusting relationship is for advisers to recognise that a thriving family business has succeeded without much guidance from advisers. In other words, it is not ill. It is, however, worried about the future, so there has to be some merit in helping the family and the business to imagine a better future and then in ensuring that advice from all advisers is aligned towards achieving the family's version of success. This is certainly a different marketing message from emphasising a current or future illness. It is an approach that can build trust without needing to scare family businesses, which is worth considering unless advisers only want to work for seriously ill family businesses and those who either are hypochondriacs or share the adviser's pessimism about the future.

Who do you trust?

The answer to the deceptively simple question, "Who do you trust?" is key to understanding how a trusting relationship forms between a family business and its adviser. In broad terms,[3] some families and advisers will prefer to trust people who are like them; while others will adopt a generally trusting attitude to everyone and not just people with whom they have some shared characteristics. It is important to be aware of the pros and cons of the different attitudes, because this will affect how family businesses and advisers trust each other and work together.

1. The 'in-group' attitude

The 'in-group' attitude to trust can be summed up as: "We trust people we know or who have something in common with us."

The shared characteristics of the group could limit those who are assumed to be trustworthy to direct family and close friends or extend to members of the same cultural, ethnic or kinship group. It could also include those advisers with whom members of the family share either an educational or professional background or some other social connection, such as membership of a club or association.

3 This is based on Eric M Uslaner, *The Moral Foundations of Trust* (New York: Cambridge UP, 2002).

"The 'in-group' attitude to trust can be summed up as: 'We trust people we know or who have something in common with us.'"

Most of us are part of in-groups and these contribute to our sense of identity because membership naturally generates an insider/outsider mentality. Insiders are people with whom we have an attachment and who it is assumed can be trusted because of this shared identity. Outsiders are strangers who should not be trusted unless they are very carefully vetted or can be monitored and controlled; but even then, insiders may still find it difficult to trust outsiders completely. A consequence of this attitude is that trust beyond the in-group tends to develop slowly, if at all, and outsiders are generally treated with suspicion.

The in-group attitude is the basis of much business networking. Family businesses and advisers often seek to exploit their respective family and social networks for commercial gain because they assume that they are networking among people who have a bias in favour of trusting them. Sometimes this entails seeking to join or gain acceptance by a group that includes potential contacts whose trust could lead to business opportunities. However, this does not always work as intended and the schmoozing fails because outsiders who are seen as seeking to gain advantage by imitating the characteristics of the in-group are viewed by actual insiders as displaying the type of insincerity that is branded as untrustworthy.

2. Limitations of the in-group attitude

The potential limitations of an in-group attitude for a family business choosing advisers is illustrated by the case of Neroli.[4] This manufacturer and distributor of leather goods was founded in Istanbul by Ishmael Karov in the late 1990s after he emigrated with his family from Bulgaria to Turkey. His wife joined him in the business; then he made his brothers partners in the firm; and as the business expanded, he involved more distant relatives, such as aunts, uncles, cousins and some close friends of the family, and then people from the same immigrant community. The underlying assumption seems to have been that they could all be trusted. But as the enterprise grew, the selection bias in favour of the in-group resulted in the family business not having access to the skilled professionals it needed in accounting, marketing and IT.

When this situation arises in family businesses with an in-group attitude to trust, it cannot be assumed that they will abandon their instinct and start hiring staff or using advisers who are outsiders. Instead, the family business could be willing to trade off the value of potentially better help or advice from outsiders against the peace of mind that comes from the business employing or being advised by insiders who can be trusted implicitly. This is an understandable compromise, but one that should be made with a clear mind. If the family business prefers advisers from its in-group who are less skilled than better-qualified outsiders, it should not complain if the advice it receives occasionally turns out to be less valuable and useful.

The problems arising from the in-group attitude to trust can be a lot worse than the above, as shown by cases of affinity fraud where a fraudster deliberately preys upon a shared group identity. The worst example of this so far in US history is Bernie Madoff, who defrauded billions of dollars from thousands of investors.

Madoff was chairman of Bernard L Madoff Investment Securities LLC from 1960 until his arrest in December 2008. His brother Peter was the senior managing director and chief compliance officer. Peter's daughter was the firm's attorney and rules and compliance officer, and Bernie's two sons were also employed in the family business.

Madoff's in-group attitude to trust is evident in how he organised and ran his business, but he also exploited his social connections to court investments from individuals and institutions among the Jewish community. Some of his clients seem to have relied on their shared background with Madoff to overcome any doubts they had about the

4 N Karra, P Tracey and N Phillips (2006), "Altruism and Agency in the Family Firm: Exploring the Role of Family, Kinship, and Ethnicity", *Entrepreneurship Theory and Practice*, 30: 861–877.

barely believable financial returns that were promised. Investors, it seems, were persuaded that it was plausible that someone from the same community or in-group could be trusted to give them a great deal on investment returns that would have sounded too good to be true had it been offered by an outsider without such ties.

Even the Madoff case, however, will not necessarily persuade family businesses with an in-group attitude that this is a risky way to conduct business with their advisers. Instead, it could be taken to illustrate how those with an in-group attitude react to breaches of trust. Violations by insiders, as in the case of Madoff, are likely to be punished severely by a breakdown of relationships and ultimately by the untrustworthy fraudster being expelled from the in-group. This means that an insider becomes an outsider and the overall attitude to trust among the continuing insiders is reinforced, rather than being damaged. In the context of this report, if a family business with an in-group attitude engages an outsider as its adviser who then lets it down in some way, the consequence could be that this reminds the family that it is better not to trust outsiders in the first place.

3. The optimists

'Optimist' is used here to describe people with a propensity to trust – those who believe that if they adopt a trusting attitude, it will be reciprocated rather than abused. Optimists no doubt assess various shared characteristics when choosing advisers, but their judgement of people does not rely primarily on these traits.

As a result, optimists are generally quicker to form and maintain trusting relationships without being constrained by the sense of vulnerability that makes those with an in-group attitude take things slowly whenever it is necessary to trust outsiders. Optimists find it easier to work with strangers without the same level of checking or controls needed to convince anyone with an in-group attitude that an outsider can be trusted.

A family with an optimist's attitude will feel comfortable trusting an adviser even if he or she is not part of the same in-group. If shared characteristics between the family business and the adviser matter at all, they will come near the end of a list of other attributes that are considered to be more important, such as the competence of the adviser or the economic cost of his or her services. The intrinsic optimism in this attitude usually means that setbacks involving breach of trust by either an adviser or a family business are absorbed without anyone sacrificing the view that people are generally trustworthy and that this attitude is the right way to live and conduct business.

Optimists would object to being described as gullible and credulous, although they are likely to be criticised in this way by those who feel more comfortable with an in-group attitude. Optimists would retort that the in-group is not immune from being cheated or defrauded by one of its own, such as in the case of Madoff. Indeed, they would argue that the in-group attitude is unduly restrictive when it comes to doing business. They would probably feel that an optimist's attitude to trust is pragmatic in a rapidly changing world where, as business and family life becomes more complex, there is not enough time always to build advisory relationships based mainly on shared in-group characteristics. Indeed, a family business selecting trusted advisers from the same in-group could become challenging as future generations grow up and often grow apart to some extent. In international families, it will be increasingly difficult to build a relationship based on an in-group attitude when there is little direct contact among some family members, let alone between them and their advisers.

4. How attitudes affect relationships

In-group supporters and optimists are each likely to argue that their attitude to trust is better, by comparing the advantages that they think their attitude offers with the disadvantages they perceive in the other. The more practical question, however, is how the different attitudes to trust matter in practice.

"Optimists are people with a propensity to trust – those who believe that if they adopt a trusting attitude, it will be reciprocated."

Families and advisers who lean strongly towards the optimist's end of the spectrum will feel uncomfortable relying on shared in-group characteristics as a decisive factor in agreeing to work together because this feels to them like an irrational bias when making such an important decision. As already mentioned, if it matters at all, the in-group identity comes near the end of a list of other attributes that are considered to be more important, such as experience, competence, price and so on.

Some families and advisers with this optimist's attitude might go so far as to say that they would prefer to have little in common with each other beyond whatever professional connection and relationship is needed to get the job done. In essence, they see merit in having a fixed boundary between their professional relationships and their personal lives. They might even not be too bothered about liking each other without this meaning that they cannot trust each other in the domain of the adviser's services. This might strike some as an arid, unattractive relationship; but that does not diminish the point that it is a relationship based on an attitude to trust that rates elements such as competence highly and attributes little value to a shared group identity.

Others, still with an optimistic bias in deciding who to trust, might be less explicit about having a boundary that separates the domains of business life and personal relationships. They would acknowledge that it is helpful for the family business and its adviser to have something in common, but they would still see social interaction outside the professional relationship as an add-on and be vigilant in avoiding negative spill-over from the personal domain into professional and business life.

Neither the family nor the adviser, for example, would expect preferential business terms from each other based on a personal connection; nor would any social obligations deter them from criticising each other for any failings. They might share a desire to ensure that the adviser's independence is preserved by him or her not forming too close a relationship with anyone in the family business which could be perceived as biased by others, making them less willing to trust the adviser. For example, if the adviser is a personal friend and confidant of the senior generation, the next generation could view this close connection as unhealthy – perhaps bordering on a conflict of interest that impedes their willingness to trust the adviser.

The above will trouble those who feel that the essence of a trusted adviser is one who has a special personal bond with the family business. This will be felt most keenly by those who now recognise that they have an in-group attitude to trust. Advisers and family businesses with this attitude will welcome the opportunity to spend time together in business and social domains because they feel that this overlap contributes to a cohesive and closer relationship. Advisers and members of the family business may be expected to attend each other's family celebrations and the adviser might even be told that he or she is "almost one of the family".

Family businesses with an in-group attitude might even accept the potential drawback that their attitude makes it more challenging to grow their business unless the advisory talent they need can be sourced from the in-group. Advisers and families in favour of sticking with the in-group attitude might argue the following:

- They feel secure in trusting one of their own for advice and this provides peace of mind.
- This relationship generates desirable psychological returns. Family and advisers feel confident that they can rely on each other and this encourages personal qualities such as empathy and sympathy.

These are impressive gains for those with an in-group attitude; but of course, optimists would claim that they can secure all these benefits doing trust their way and the only difference is that they are willing to trust outsiders who are rejected by those with an in-group mind set. This simply reiterates that both attitudes to trust can work; but knowing that there are different attitudes gives family businesses and advisers an insight into how they can strategically deploy trust in their relationship. Put simply, those with the same attitude are more likely to enjoy working together. However, both optimists and in-group adherents will at least agree that there is a lot to be gained by mobilising trust in building their relationship – advantages that are beyond the understanding of those who denigrate the notion that trust is an effective way to do business.

Trusting a shared purpose

Why would a family want to start a business or stay in business together?

Why would people decide to spend part of their life working with relatives or being in a relationship of financial interdependence with them as owners of a business?

If advisers do not know a family's answers to these questions, what assumptions will they make when advising a family business and the individual family members?

But if advisers do not know why a family wants to be in business together, how can their advice be trusted when it is based on assumptions that may well be mistaken?

1. The risk of assumptions

The shared purpose in a family business is the set of goals that the family is striving to achieve through being in business together. These represent the family's unique version of success, against which it will measure its overall achievements and, it is reasonable to assume, the value of help provided by advisers. The shared purpose will be based on the family's traditions and culture, along with its aspirations for the future of the business and of the family, both as individuals and as a unit.

The variety of goals that could form the shared purpose of a family business is challenging for advisers to fully understand, so it is helpful for them to know that research shows that while families consistently prioritise financial concerns, they also consider non-financial objectives to be highly important.[5] The non-financial returns on investment (ROIs) to which a family might attribute value include the following:

- stewarding assets and passing on the business to successive generations;
- looking after various stakeholder interests, such as employees, customers and suppliers;
- keeping the family connected with each other through an interest in the business as individual family members follow their own lifestyles;
- maintaining overall family harmony;
- providing career opportunities for family members in an uncertain world;
- being involved in a particular type of business activity to which the family feels passionately attached;
- putting something back into a local community or society generally by creating jobs or through philanthropy, or by engaging in other social or political activities;
- maintaining a positive image and respect for the family that is connected to its members being known as business owners and, for some, being business leaders; and
- encouraging entrepreneurship and risk taking among family members by providing them with resources, such as financial capital and social connections, in order to pursue their own ambitions.

It can be argued that this information supports a common-sense view that should be accepted without the need for much debate, which is that every family business will have a shared purpose that is unique to that family and includes some combination of financial and non-financial ROIs. However, advisers may choose to ignore this and instead make other assumptions in order to give direction to their advice.

There is a tendency for advisers to absorb the prevailing attitudes or assumptions of their profession because career advancement is to some extent a trek towards conformity; but it is worrying if such assumptions become so embedded that advisers lose the ability, or even the desire, to consider the possibility that they may be implausible as the basis for advising some family businesses. For

5 GT Lumpkin, L Steier and M Wright (2011), "Strategic Entrepreneurship in Family Business", *Strategic Entrepreneurship Journal*, Vol 5 Issue 4, 285-306.

example, the purpose of every family business, it may be assumed, is to balance financial ROIs for the current generation with preserving wealth for future generations through mitigating the taxes paid by the business and the family. While these goals will accurately describe the shared purpose of some family businesses, and to some extent matter for many family businesses, it is wrong to assume that this amounts to the shared purpose of every family business.

For example, there are some families that accept paying tax as the cost of living in a civilised society. Others want to encourage entrepreneurial risk taking in each generation in order to build a fortune that is capable of serving the interests of a larger family in the future. In doing this, the family accepts the implicit risk of loss of money and even of family reputation if a new venture fails. This desire to take risks and create wealth describes part of the motivation of every entrepreneur; and if a family wants the next generation to think and act entrepreneurially, it will be frustrated by the idea that wealth preservation for future generations is more important than current wealth creation. It would point out that wealth preservation is not the way to build a business, and that an aversion to taking commercial risks in favour of preserving wealth could in fact create the risk of a business not growing fast enough to support a growing family.

"The notion that wealth preservation is a priority for every family business may be accepted by advisers, unquestioningly and wrongly, as a stated fact of human behaviour. This mind set might in turn give life to another common assumption that could be criticised as reflecting an anti-family bias among advisers: that the best way to preserve the family business is to assume that the next generation should not be entirely trusted."

The notion that wealth preservation is a priority for every family business may be accepted by advisers, unquestioningly and wrongly, as a stated fact of human behaviour. This mind set might in turn give life to another common assumption that could be criticised as reflecting an anti-family bias among advisers: that the best way to preserve the family business is to assume that the next generation should not be entirely trusted.

Relying, it seems, on a combination of well-known clichés about the inevitable decline of a family business over the span of three generations and data about the increasing occurrence of relationship breakdowns, advisers recommend technical structures to protect the family business from the family. In such cases one might expect an adviser who wishes to be trusted by the family to verify that the family agrees with the assumptions that the next generation – who often have been parented and educated with care and at some expense – will all be stupid and lazy, bound to be involved in unsuccessful personal relationships and incapable of looking after the family business. But how often are these assumptions verified with the client?

The advisers might argue that their assumptions in favour of wealth preservation and tax mitigation are partly in response to the client's instructions to "keep it simple". In order to do this and provide advice for a reasonable fee, the adviser cannot afford to explore the more nuanced set of reasons about why a family wants to stay in business together. While it is easy to sympathise with the goal of simplicity, members of a family business might later wonder why they are confused by the way advisers produce complex technical structures and even occasionally manage to disagree among themselves, using obscure jargon, over which specialist answer is the best way of implementing the instructions to keep it simple.

As well as being a disservice to family business clients, advisers who base advice on over-simplistic and potentially erroneous assumptions sow seeds of distrust among a family, which cannot be faulted for wondering, "Does this adviser really understand us, or even want to understand us?" The adviser is also missing an interesting opportunity to help a family business achieve its very personal overall ROI as expressed in its shared purpose, as illustrated in the following example.

2. Working with a shared purpose

This second-generation family business is owned equally by four siblings, two of whom work in the business. One of them is trusted by the other family members as the CEO. There are nine cousins in the third generation, ranging from nine to 32 years of age. The complexity of the business is making the siblings feel that for the first time, they might need to recruit non-family to fill senior roles in the business; but they would still like the next CEO, if possible, to be a family member. It is important for the siblings to agree a shared purpose that can be explained to the next generation and to any outsider who might be admitted to a position of trust in helping to manage the family business. The siblings, therefore, agree the following five-pronged shared purpose for their family business:

- *Provide reasonable financial security for a growing family:* In the family's opinion, this means a predictable dividend per share based on a percentage of annual net profits subject to a minimum below which the dividend cannot fall. The minimum gives family owners the level of financial security which they feel is desirable and which is also considered to represent a reasonable cost of capital for the business without it being put under financial stress. As the family grows and shares are more widely distributed among the next generation, the siblings want the total amount that the business pays as dividend to increase in order to provide this level of financial security for a growing family.
- *Preserve a legacy of owning this particular business that trades under the family name:* Bound up in this aim is the reputation of the business for providing quality products at affordable prices, which is represented by using the family name as a brand. This also means, however, that the family's status, reputation and social standing are all affected by how the business conducts its affairs, and vice versa.
- *Remain connected to the local area where the family's business has always been located:* The siblings think that this is part of what of others now call corporate social responsibility. They feel that their commitment to keeping the business in the local area is reciprocated in long-term service by employees who are reasonably confident about their job security. This pattern of long service has helped to build know-how in the workplace and avoid the disruption caused by high levels of staff turnover. The siblings often repeat one of the sayings of their late father who founded the business: "This is not just our family business; it is a business of many families."
- *Keep ownership in the hands of direct bloodline descendants and pass ownership to the next generation:* This reflects the family's overall sense of stewardship. The siblings feel that they have a better chance of achieving continuity of their family's legacy if ownership is restricted to bloodline family members. The goal of passing ownership to the next generation also reflects a feeling among the current owners that since they inherited shares from their mother and father, rather than investing their own cash in the business, the shares are not for sale and the next generation of cousins should be

"It is important to agree a shared purpose that can be explained to the next generation and to any outsider who might be admitted to a position of trust in helping to manage the family business."

given an opportunity to inherit the rights and responsibilities of ownership.

- *Ideally, appoint one of the family to lead the business:* To this end, the siblings want to encourage family members to pursue a career in the business and have agreed that they would prefer a reasonably competent family member to be the next CEO rather than a better-qualified outsider. This was not an easy decision, since it involved coming to terms with the possibility that appointing one of their own over a better-qualified outsider might diminish the returns available for the first objective of achieving reasonable financial security for a growing family. But the trade-off feels right for this family, and it is committed to the task of trying to ensure that a next-generation family member will assume leadership of the business. For this family, peace of mind as an ROI involves a relative being in charge of running the business.

It does not matter what advisers think of this shared purpose, because it is not their shared purpose. If any adviser feels strongly that the family is wrong headed in pursuing this set of ambitions, he or she should decline to act and certainly must not replace the shared purpose with whatever assumptions the adviser thinks are somehow better. What the family business needs are different specialists who can be trusted to collaborate in translating the shared purpose into the constitutional documents for the company and arranging the private affairs of each family owner.

After discussing the shared purpose, the family's trusted advisers come back with the following comments in order to confirm that the family understands the consequences of its choices:

- Owners will be expected to hold on to shares and pass a legacy to the next generation by way of a gift. This means that for the moment, sale of the company is off the table.
- Owners will be unable to transfer shares to anyone who is not a bloodline relative, which excludes spouses or partners from becoming owners. The siblings accept that they each now need to ensure that their personal will complies with this requirement.
- It will be important for the owners that the board ensures that shares in the company always qualify for whatever tax reliefs are available in relation to passing shares to the next generation as a gift.
- There will be a limited market if an owner wants to sell shares, because of both the bloodline rule and the sense of stewardship, meaning that shares are not meant to be a tradable investment. The only people who can buy shares are other current owners or those who are eligible to become owners in the future.

- For these reasons, the price in the event of any share sale between relatives is unlikely to be full market value, which reflects the above points and the underlying feeling that "the shares are not really mine to sell".
- Owners must understand the dividend policy and not expect more income from their shares.
- Overall, therefore, the owners have a relatively illiquid investment that gives a reasonable financial return which is balanced by the other, non-financial returns that the family values as expressed in its shared purpose.

The advisers also raise other points for the family to consider. For example, they ask whether the family's strong views on bloodline ownership mean that the trustees, as well as the beneficiaries, of any trust that may hold shares in the company should be limited to bloodline family who are eligible to become shareholders. This would mean that outsiders, including professional advisers, could not be appointed as trustees, which sounds right to the family. The family further agrees that a similar restriction should apply to shareholder proxies so that an owner who is unable to attend a shareholders' meeting can appoint as proxy only someone else who is either a shareholder or eligible to become an owner, and not an outsider.

These decisions prompt the siblings to agree that 25 years is the minimum age at which the next generation can become an owner, a proxy or a trustee of a trust. They also agree that they should aim to transfer all their shares before their 75th birthday, to avoid the business becoming a gerontocracy. By this age, the shareholders should have been able to make personal financial arrangements so as not to miss the dividends that they would then no longer receive.

This helpful exchange spurs the family to ask what would happen if one of the next generation did not have children: would he or she have to sell the shares or could they be gifted to bloodline relatives in another branch of the family? If the shares were to be valued for the purpose of sale at a low price as mentioned earlier, it could be unfair for a shareholder, or the executors of his or her will, to be forced to sell the shares at a discounted value simply because he or she did not have children.

What about any shareholder without children making a gift of shares as the way out of a possible ownership cul-de-sac created by the family's shared purpose? At this point, the siblings acknowledge that the balance of power among them is based on each branch of the family having 25% of the share capital. The siblings consider no branch having overall control to be healthy for the family and the business, since everyone has to accept that compromise and getting along with their relatives is the pragmatic way to enjoy the benefits of being an owner. They had assumed that this balance of power among the four branches would continue in future generations; but a gift across branches would cause a change. One solution might be for the company to buy back shares, but it is understood that this cannot be guaranteed to be viable whenever it might be needed. There needs to be some more thinking by this family before the rules on ownership are finally settled, which is good news for advisers who enjoy such challenges.

Moving on to the business, the shared purpose means that the business plan must be about steady growth to generate reasonable returns for a growing family, and doing this while remaining connected to the local area and preferably by having a family member in charge of leading the business. The desire to have a reasonable dividend that increases in aggregate as the number of owners increases in the next generation must be expressed in a set of growth targets for the business. The business needs to grow at a rate that generates the dividend that gives the family its desired level of financial security. The family also prefers dividends to be covered by annual profits and not reserves, and to be funded by positive cash, which means that the board cannot borrow money to pay dividends to the shareholders.

The family thinks that this dividend policy is reasonable and reflects its inherited values in relation to debt. The family explains to the advisers that during the founders' era, the company almost went bust after borrowing too much money to grow the business. The family now wants to fund growth through retained earnings and thinks that its dividend expectations are reasonable given that members have to lock their capital into the business and cannot sell shares. This gives management the benefit of secure and affordable capital with which to run the business. While the siblings are happy to provide patient capital, they are not passive investors and think that the targets for dividends and growth will help to keep the business reasonably healthy.

The targets in any incentive plan for management in this family business cannot involve shares, as ownership is restricted to bloodline. The incentives need to be aligned to the family's strong views on what is acceptable as an overall ROI as expressed in the shared purpose. If management, for example, tried to achieve other targets, such as maximising short-term profits through saving costs by relocating the business and making redundancies, it would not be long before the relationship between the owners and the business leaders became very strained.

This is a reminder of why the family wants one of its own in the position of CEO: that person could be trusted implicitly to honour the shared purpose even in the absence of a formal incentive plan, although the siblings also accept that a plan is needed to recruit and retain non-family to work in the business. This leads the siblings to agree that it would be a good idea to have a clear policy that encourages the next generation to join the family business and aim for the boardroom. A draft of this policy will be prepared by one of the advisers who is an employment law specialist and will then be discussed by the siblings before it is presented in draft to the next generation for their feedback.

While the family feels more comfortable with the idea of a relative being in charge of the business, it also wants some restraints on the decision-making power of the board. The family believes that the 'big decisions' that go to the heart of its shared purpose should always be made by the owners rather than the board, so they agree that in future the following will all need to be approved by the holders of a simple majority of the shares:

- any large investments that could represent a significant commercial risk for the owners;
- any changes to the dividend policy;
- any decision to incur debt;
- any decision to relocate the premises or make any redundancies;

"As well as inheriting a share of the family business, the next generation may feel that they have inherited a responsibility to abide by the shared purpose set by their ancestors."

- any change to the company name or brand, since these are the family names and so affect the reputation and standing of the family; and
- any corporate sponsorships, because again these use the family name.

It is reasonable to ask why ambitious advisers would ever want to deny themselves the interesting challenge of understanding a family's shared purpose and translating it into effective governance for the family and its business. Surely, advisers who seek to understand a shared purpose are far more likely to gain and retain the trust of a family business than advisers who choose to ignore the shared purpose and replace it with other assumptions?

The following practical issues pertain to the task of creating a good enough shared purpose:

- Who is trusted to decide the shared purpose?
- What if there is no shared purpose?

3. Who is the client?
At its best, a shared purpose represents a voluntary commitment by members of a family to be in business together. Some families and advisers believe that planning for the future of a family business should involve only the current family owners; while others believe that it should engage as many as possible of those who will be affected by the outcome, such as the next generation, the wider family of spouses and partners and any key non-family personnel in the business.

Those who focus on the current owners argue – reasonably enough – that they can do whatever they want with their share of the family business, subject only to any interests or claims that they either have to or choose to recognise. The adviser and the family members who work together on this basis may discuss whether to inform the next generation of the eventual plan, as distinct from involving them in the planning. However, sometimes concern about the impact on heirs of knowing too much about their future wealth results in plans being kept from them – at least until they reach a designated age by which they are expected to be more mature. Presumably, when the heirs receive news of their inheritance, it is perceived as a blessing that enables them to.... Do what, exactly? Does it provide them with the means to follow their own aspirations and career choices, or will it determine these choices for them?

As well as inheriting a share of the family business, the next generation may feel that they have inherited a responsibility to abide by the shared purpose set by their ancestors. For example, if the ancestors dreamed of a multi-generational family business and advisers put in place technical structures to achieve this goal, an heir who later would prefer to sell the business and pursue his or her own life aspirations will have little, if any, opportunity to fulfil this ambition. This is a situation that is unlikely to be happy for either the owner or the business that, due to this planning, now has to cope with a permanently dissatisfied owner.

By way of a fuller example, assume that the current owners of the family business with a strong work ethic believe that ownership should be restricted to bloodline family members who work in the business. They feel that this will help to avoid resentment among working owners that their efforts are profiting owners who do not contribute to the business by the sweat of their brows. With this in mind, the advisers to the current owners put in place suitably restrictive rules for ownership.

This decision, however, could have unintended consequences for the next generation. Family members who decide to pursue other careers and are cut out of ownership may feel that they are also being cut off from the family, especially if the business represents a significant portion of the family's wealth and reputation. Alternatively, they might opt to join the family business in order to qualify for ownership, but resent that they are being forced into making this career decision. This is why prescribing that owners must work in the family business is sometimes described as creating a set of golden handcuffs.

The alternative approach to setting the family's shared purpose is to involve everyone of adult age – or at least maturity, since the two are not always correlated – who will be affected by whatever shared purpose is ultimately agreed. A broader discussion about why it wants to remain in business together can be challenging for a family, since outright honesty is not always possible or in some cases acceptable for cultural reasons. However, this type of discussion at least creates the opportunity for a family to work together towards a consensus that balances the past with the future needs and ambitions of the family and the business. This might also be preferable for the adviser who, having a longer-term and healthy sense of self-interest, wants to be trusted by the next generation of family owners and leaders.

The idea of the shared purpose of the family business being decided in each generation by a larger group of stakeholders is a new paradigm that has the benefit of at least reflecting life's realities from the perspective of family businesses. Every individual will know intuitively that his or her personal decisions will affect, and be affected by, the decisions taken by other relatives. While there is no doubt that effective planning for a family business must take account of a number

"The idea of the shared purpose of the family business being decided in each generation by a larger group of stakeholders has the benefit of reflecting life's realities."

of distinct and competing interests, working with this larger stakeholder group will give some advisers concerns over confidentiality and possible conflicts of interest. Each profession needs to decide how to deal with its professional rules governing these matters; and with so many professions providing advice to family business clients, it is impossible to give a comprehensive review of the relevant guidelines as part of this special report.

Whether the trusted adviser works with the current owners or the wider family to agree and then implement a shared purpose, the adviser faces the challenge of having to offer candid and independent advice that is not affected by extraneous factors, such as a relationship with particular family members. It is understandable for advisers to be attracted to the family members who are currently in power, given that they decide which advisers to use and how much to pay as fees; but this relationship may be viewed as biased by others in the family, including the next generation who one day will become owners. Such conflicts of interest are a matter of perception for every adviser to manage, but they undoubtedly can corrode, rather than enhance, the relationship of trust between an adviser and the wider family.

These issues become more acute if the adviser accepts a fiduciary position in relation to the family business, such as a director or trustee, where the legal duties that are owed to certain individuals or groups may clash with the expectations of different family stakeholders. In advising a family business, the trusted advisers may have to accept that independence means being independent of any other role in the family business and ensuring that other relationships are not perceived as warping their ability to treat different family interests as being equally important.

The topic of conflict of interest could affect family members as much as it concerns some advisers. It is common to find individual family members with different roles in the family and the business. The same person, for example, could be a shareholder, trustee, director, employee, parent, spouse, sibling or cousin; and when wearing these different hats, he or she may struggle to decide what to do. There could well be a clash between the legal obligations to fulfil different types of fiduciary duties as a director and as a trustee, and the decision that must be taken in either of these roles might be different from what the person feels is in the best interests of his or her loved ones; and in the midst of all these choices there is a small, insistent voice saying, "But what about me?"

"Advisers often equate success with the continuity of a particular business, which implies that those who do not achieve this outcome are failures. This is narrow minded."

4. What if there is no shared purpose? (The cult of continuity)
Which of the following cases deserves to be classified as a failure?

- A group of siblings sell their parents' business after deciding they would get on better as family if they were not in business together.
- An entrepreneur decides to sell her businesses and give her children from different marriages money to start their own businesses and make their own mistakes, while also leaving a substantial charitable endowment for the extended family to run together.
- A family of 35 bloodline relatives in three branches decides to partition the business so that two branches each take over one of the two commercial businesses and the other branch moves into cash, a substantial portion of which is initially loaned to one of the other family branches to aid the transition and, after repayment, is used to fund a family office.

Advisers to family businesses often equate success with continuity of a particular business, which implies that those who do not achieve this outcome – such as the examples above – are failures. This is both mean spirited and narrow minded. The cult of continuity is expressed in the data that claims to show that only a small percentage of family businesses survive the transition between generations. It is a story told through the conventional narratives of 'clogs to clogs' or 'shirtsleeves to shirtsleeves' in three generations; of how unworthy and untalented successors consume a fortune to fund lifestyles or seek social or political distinction, rather than concentrating on growing the family's business. The message is that so many families failing to continue their current businesses beyond the third generation is a crisis, apparently.

No, it is not.

Not everyone wants to devote part of their adult years linked by a partial or total financial dependence on their relatives or to remain connected with them through a shared interest in the family business. Sale of the family business should not be defined as failure; nor should a business being wound up due to market conditions or because the family members no longer wish to support it with their financial and human capital. Families that choose not to continue their businesses do so for whatever combination of business and family reasons makes sense to them. Afterwards, some of them might start a new business or set up a family office where they remain connected through shared investments and sometimes other activities, such as funding new start-ups and philanthropy.

In other words, the families achieve a version of continuity – just not

"Is it better to celebrate the survival of the legacy business and ignore the family's wider achievements?"

one that involves continuity of their ancestors' business; but the cult of continuity would, bizarrely, record these as failures.

The cult of continuity also does not account well for the families that still own their original business, but whose success is more about how they have diversified into a range of other assets and activities. Why is it better to celebrate the survival of the legacy business and ignore, and therefore fail to understand, the family's wider achievements?

Most families want to nurture, protect and grow their wealth; but they also know that they cannot always look after a growing family by maintaining the status quo. When deciding its shared purpose, it is important that a family does not feel constrained by a fixation with longevity of one business activity as being the reason why it ought to remain in business together. Nor should advisers make this outdated version of continuity the assumption on which to base their advice.

It is important for the trusted adviser to have the courage, if need be, to conclude that there is no shared purpose among a family because members want different things from their business or in their lives. That might be hard news to convey to a family business, but it is far better than making the error of creating structures that bind them together through their business and into a life of relatively affluent misery.

In reporting the absence of a compelling shared purpose, the adviser may be articulating what everyone else is scared to admit, for fear of upsetting each other. However, if the family agrees with the adviser's conclusion, either in sadness or with a mighty sense of relief, the work going forward for the family and its trusted advisers becomes how to separate their interests with as little cost (emotional and financial) as possible.

Creating the trusted team

George Bernard Shaw described the professions as a conspiracy against the laity. Family businesses that sympathise with him are unlikely to embrace the idea of engaging a group of professional advisers to work together as a team. They will prefer a series of bilateral relationships with their advisers, maybe using different advisers for their business and family affairs to avoid the risk of any one of them knowing much more than what is needed to do his or her own specialist work. But these families are not the audience for this special report.

Nor are advisers who would admit to being sales driven, whose paramount goal is to maximise the fees from any client for the range of services that the adviser and his or her colleagues can provide. Cross-selling is their mantra; and while this is intended to be helpful by providing what is often described as a universal service, or a one-stop shop, and is understandable for advisers working in competitive markets, it is difficult to imagine that the adviser's self-interest will always equate to the best interests of a family and its business. Advisers must judge whose interests they prioritise when cross-selling and expect their clients to do the same. Families may struggle to develop a trusted relationship with advisers who they suspect want to maximise their income from fees or commissions; but the advisers are unlikely to be too bothered with this, or at best will feign concern, because they adhere to a different business model.

Self-styled realists might argue that the above describes the state we are in. The social bonds of trust and respect between family businesses and advisers have weakened and more selfish interests prevail on both sides of this relationship. Advisers are mainly interested in profits, while family businesses want more for less and are ready to sue, or change, their adviser if need be.

But it is unnecessary to accept such anomie as inevitable, however loudly the realists – or are they just pessimists? – proclaim their dismal opinions. The more optimistic view is that basing an advisory relationship on mutual trust will generate excellent revenues for advisers and deliver outstanding service for family businesses. For families and advisers who still want trust to matter in their commercial relationship, it is necessary to address the question, "How do you organise a team of trusted advisers to serve a family business?" The answer offered in this chapter might just amount to a Shavian rebuke.

1. What type of team?

The affairs of a family whose lives are connected through the shared ownership and possibly leadership of a business, plus the needs of the business itself, are too complex to be served by a single adviser, by whatever name called. The notion of the general practitioner, *homme d'affaires* or *consigliore* who does everything for the family and its business has become extinct. The modish equivalents of an individual, most trusted adviser who perhaps acts a gatekeeper between the family and other advisers is a nostalgic notion sustained in part by the desire of advisers to be closer to the family and its business than would be likely were the adviser's only engagement through his or her specialist work.

While specialists are commonplace and dominate the advisory space, they cannot work in isolation because the challenges in a family business are not entirely reducible to a series of technical problems to which individual specialist advisers can provide discrete technical answers. Most decisions or choices facing a family business will have wider repercussions that advisers will be trusted to identify and manage. For example, the simple decision to restrict ownership to bloodline family members must be followed through by the different specialists who prepare the company's constitutional documents and the wills of the existing and future owners, and in the definition of beneficiaries in any family trust that owns shares.

This reality means that specialists advising a family business already work together as a team of sorts. They share information and intermingle advice, but still mostly they contribute to the team by focusing on their respective specialist areas. This is a team that, due to the complex needs of a family business, is multi-disciplinary out of necessity; but there is a minimum of interdependence among team members beyond where the technical worlds of different specialists overlap or collide.

This multi-disciplinary advisory team is not formally constituted or managed as a team and may exhibit traits that, for many, are not that team-like. For example, there may be occasional territorial disputes as advisers and their respective firms which can provide a range of services compete with each other to gain a larger slice of advisory work from the family business. There could be poor communication among the team as individual specialists express what they consider to be important from within their specialist silo in a technical argot that other advisers, let alone the family business, struggle to understand.

This raises an interesting question as to how the members of such an advisory team trust each other. The approaches to creating a trusted relationship described earlier in this special report will apply among a multi-disciplinary group of advisers:

- Some advisers will have an in-group attitude to trust, which means that they prefer to work with other advisers with whom they have something in common. The most obvious example is the desire of advisers in the same firm to work together, thus

"Specialists cannot work in isolation because the challenges in a family business are not limited to problems to which individual specialist advisers can provide all the answers."

combining the virtue of convenience for the family and its business with increased overall income for the advisers. The other examples of an in-group attitude mentioned earlier would be where advisers rely on a shared educational or cultural background or other social connection, such as membership of a club or association, when referring work to each other.
- Other advisers, described earlier as the optimists, will be generally more trusting – while taking account of competence and perhaps some characteristics shared with other advisers, they will be prone towards making an assumption that all advisers are generally trustworthy.
- The advisers must decide how much to trust in each other's competence. This form of trust may be based on past personal experience or on an assumption that a qualified professional working for a particular organisation with a good reputation must have the necessary skills.
- Some advisers will view extending trust to professional colleagues as being part of an economic relationship whose success will be measured by other business flowing between the advisers in future.
- Another feature could be that the issue of trust is treated as a marginal matter – an approach that is underpinned by the view that if anything goes wrong, someone can always be sued.

In whatever way they come to trust each other, a group of specialists working for the same family business is multi-disciplinary born out of necessity, rather than a proper team in which the risk and reward for every individual adviser depends to some extent on the performance of the other team members.

2. Creating an advisory team

The difference between the familiar multi-disciplinary group of advisers that is created out of necessity and an inter-disciplinary advisory team requires us to identify how to organise the latter. The following issues should be considered:

- the shared purpose of the family business;
- matters to consider when appointing advisers to the team;
- how advisers are held accountable;
- the way in which the team of advisers is rewarded; and
- the style of leadership that is needed in this type of team.

In order to make the challenge more interesting, it should be assumed when considering these criteria that the specialists on the team come from different organisations; although some would argue that the challenge of getting different specialists from the same organisation to work together as a team is every bit as difficult.

3. Shared purpose

First and foremost, a team of trusted advisers each will understand what the family is striving to achieve through being in business together, which was described in the previous chapter as the family's shared purpose. Only then can the family and the advisers be confident that all advice is aligned to achieving a successful outcome as defined and understood by the family. Where uncertainty exists, advisers who wish to be trusted will take time to clarify the shared purpose and will not make assumptions, such as the conventional tropes that every family business only wants to maximise financial returns and protect wealth from being squandered by dissolute inheritors.

The trusted advisers' insistence on understanding the shared purpose for the family business is based on knowing the dangers of proceeding in the absence of such clarity. Any group of people trying to achieve different types of return from the same business is a recipe for conflict – perhaps even more so when the protagonists in this struggle are related to each other. For example, one sibling may want to maximise the exit value from selling the family business within the next five years and another may want to build a business legacy to pass to future generations; each has a noble reason for being in business, but it is unlikely that they will want to be in business together because that business will never satisfy their divergent aims. Before these siblings go much further, their trusted advisers will want reassurance that there is a shared purpose to be implemented.

4. Appointment

A functional approach based on the type of services that a family and its business need is obviously part of determining who should be on the advisory team; but the more interesting questions are who makes the appointments and the attributes of team members beyond their functional specialisms.

The simple answer to the question "Who appoints?" is the client; but who is the client for this purpose? The family business client is always a group of relatives with potentially divergent interests who own a business, some of whom may also work in the business, possibly alongside non-family senior managers who make a significant contribution to the business's success. This variety of stakeholders makes the question, "Who appoints?" rather more complicated than it first appears.

If appointments are made by those currently in power – whether that be the senior generation of the family, the majority shareholder or the board of directors – the savvy adviser will want to check that he or she will be trusted by the other stakeholders. The likes of the next generation, the minority shareholders and any non-family senior

"Appointment to the team depends on the family business having trust and confidence in the adviser. Therefore, there may be limited opportunity for advisers to delegate work to more junior personnel."

managers may each engage at some point with the advisers and represent potential sources of work for them, so it is important that they know and trust each other.

Even if the client is restricted to those who are currently in power, the trusted advisers need to consider how to address the interests of all parties who will be affected in some way by their work. This is tantamount to asking: to whom does the trusted adviser to a family business owe a duty of care?

For example, the decision made by those currently in power to restrict voting shares in the family business to the next generation who work in the business could influence the career decisions of the next generation. Some may decide that they need to work in the family business in order to qualify for shares, rather than because they want to pursue this career. If, however, the most talented in the next generation resist the lure of the wealth and power attached to ownership and choose other careers and lifestyles, the business could end up under the control of less talented relatives. It is necessary to ask whether the professional duty of care is owed only to the parties in power at the moment who like the idea of owners always working in the business, or whether it should extend to the next generation who could be affected by the outcome of the adviser's work.

Other attributes of advisers beyond specialist competence might matter when creating an interdisciplinary advisory team. The client might want diversity in the age and gender of its team to match the family demographic as a means of ensuring that the advisers overall can relate effectively to the different stakeholder interests in the family and the business. They may also want team members to demonstrate the following characteristics before they are appointed:

- show respect for the shared purpose of the family business and be able to illustrate clearly in a way the client understands how this will be implemented within the adviser's domain of expertise;
- understand that the interests of the different stakeholders in the family business are simultaneously independent and intertwined and be able to explain how they will represent these individual and collective needs;
- enjoy presenting complex ideas clearly in ways that are within the grasp of the different stakeholders and do not seek refuge in obscure technical jargon;
- communicate openly with, rather than behind the backs of, those who own and lead the family business or other team members;
- be able to give and take constructive criticism to or from the client and other advisers on the team;

- do not sulk if the family ignores advice;
- do not need to win every argument or enhance their sense of self-worth by trying to appear as the smartest people in the room;
- respect boundaries around who provides which advisory services and avoid unproductive competition among team members that is aimed at securing more of the client's work at the expense of another team member;
- have a healthy sense of self-interest that is enlightened by a commitment to the family's shared purpose and to other members of the advisory team;
- display an independent mind set that is not affected or swayed by relationships with any of the stakeholders in the family business or with other team members; and
- retain independence and be wary of accepting any positions that create a conflict of interest. Such a conflict will arise, for example, where an adviser accepts another role such as shareholder, trustee of a family trust or director on the board of the family business, because each of these creates a different interest or duty for the adviser that could conflict with the primary role of being trusted by the family and its business to give independent advice.

Since appointment to the team depends on the family business having trust and confidence in the adviser's character and skills, there may be limited opportunity for any of the advisers to delegate execution of their work to more junior personnel. This might be awkward for an adviser whose business model separates doing professional work from managing the client relationship and assumes that the former is delegable. Some clients will enjoy and value the attention bestowed on them by the adviser who wants to manage relationships as a distinct service; while others will feel that this is unnecessary and wonder how the cost of the relationship manager's investment of time is being recovered, with a profit, through fees and other charges. Family businesses which believe that ultimately they pay for everything might perceive a lack of transparency in the cost of relationship building by the client relationship manager – especially if they assume that the main aim of these efforts is to maximise revenue opportunities for the adviser's business.

The family business which is against its trusted advisers delegating work might have to pay more for the reassurance of the chosen adviser doing work personally that, on the basis of the skills needed, could be delegated. However, this will be balanced by the value the family perceives in the adviser developing a long-term, deep relationship with it and its business through being involved in the to and fro of executing work, and the reassurance of knowing that the

"The ultimate objective for the advisory team is to help the family and its business achieve the shared purpose."

family is in the safe hands of someone who has been carefully selected to be a trusted member of the advisory team.

An adviser who is concerned that this level of commitment to the team runs counter to his or her commercial self-interest might want to argue the following:

- The team is mission driven – the ultimate aim being to implement the shared purpose – rather than task driven.
- The role of the trusted adviser in overseeing particular tasks or transactions executed by more junior colleagues is overall a more effective way of fulfilling the shared purpose.

The above considerations make the answer to the question, "Who appoints?" more interesting than it first appears, but the entire question may be swept aside where advisory relationships are inherited along with the family business. The administration of technical structures around ownership of the business and other family wealth may tie a family to a particular adviser or organisation not as a matter of choice, but just because the effort and cost of disentangling the advisory connections make the family feel this is not worthwhile. This highlights the importance of the family and the business being clear about how they will hold their advisory team accountable.

5. Accountability

The best way to hold a team of advisers accountable is to start with what counts for the family business and then find a way to count it.

Since the ultimate objective for the advisory team is to help the family and its business to achieve the shared purpose, the team should have a set of goals that are the technical expression of that shared purpose. Goal setting is commonplace in business and some also use it in private life, so there should be no controversy in using it to channel the efforts of the different advisers on a team to achieving the shared purpose that motivates the family to be in business together. By way of example, the shared purpose discussed in "Trusting a shared purpose" is summarised in Table 2 alongside high-level goals for the advisory team.

These broad goals can be broken down further into tasks for each adviser on the team. This will help to establish who does what – in particular, in relation to any services that could be provided by more than one adviser on the team. Clarifying these boundaries and ensuring that they are respected in practice are vital to the success of the advisory team.

It is regularly claimed that the process of goal setting will help to bind a team together and enhance the shared sense of commitment, which in this case is a commitment to help the family business to achieve its shared purpose. A rigorous approach to goal setting will help to avoid the risk of advisers pursuing other incompatible goals – which, interestingly, could include those being used to measure the adviser's performance in his or her host organisation. For example, while an adviser being expected to cross-sell other services makes good business sense for his or her organisation, this should not be allowed to breach the agreed boundaries around who does what on the team of trusted advisers.

The topic of accountability extends to considering the extent to which the team is collectively responsible for achieving the shared purpose. Some would argue that an adviser can only be responsible, or culpable, for his or her own performance, and not for the performance of others on the team. The alternative to this individualistic view would be that the advisory team that takes on the complexity of a family business must be committed to coordinating how work is conducted, and that this results in collective responsibility for the outcome. The deciding factor in the matter is, of course, the family's expectations rather than the preferences of advisers; but there is a strong *prima facie* case that a team that is being held collectively responsible has a strong reason to ensure that every member is playing by the rules that are in place to enhance overall team performance.

Table 2. Family business's shared purpose and corresponding goals for advisory team

Shared purpose	High-level goals for advisers
To provide reasonable financial security for a growing family In the family's opinion, this means a predictable dividend per share based on a percentage of annual net profits subject to a minimum below which the dividend cannot fall; the dividend must also be paid from positive cash flow.	Establish how to calculate the minimum dividend that the family wants and help to create a financial model that balances the family's expectations with the needs of the business for reinvestment, including considering an overall reasonable cost of capital for the business benchmarked with comparable businesses. Help family members with personal financial and tax planning so that they achieve whatever reasonable financial security means for them.
To preserve a legacy of owning this particular business that trades under the family name Bound up in this aim is the reputation of the business for providing quality products at affordable prices, which is promoted by using the family name as a brand.	Ensure that the trademark or brand is properly protected. Consider decisions regarding use of the brand by the business being subject to family approval. Create protocols to help the family avoid behaviours that could adversely affect the brand. Ensure that any PR concerning the brand is shared with family members, since it involves their family name and reputation.
To remain connected to the local area where the family's business has always been located The family feels that its commitment to keeping the business in the local area is reciprocated in long-term service by employees who are reasonably confident about their job security.	Suggest how real estate used in the business is held so that the family, and not the board, controls decisions about this property. Determine how the family can control decisions to relocate the business. Help the business to scan developments in local planning laws and local politics to gain early warning of anything that could affect the family's attachment to this location. Ensure that employment policies incentivise and reward the long-term commitment that the family values.

continued on next page

Shared purpose	High-level goals for advisers
Ownership always to be in the hands of direct bloodline descendants of the founder and to pass to the next generation The family feels it has a better chance of achieving continuity of its legacy if ownership is restricted to bloodline family members.	Ensure that the constitution of the business and the personal affairs of every shareholder are consistent with this restriction on ownership. This includes the terms of any trust created to hold shares.
Ideally, for one of the family to lead the business The family wants to encourage family members to pursue a career in the business and has agreed that a reasonably competent family member would be preferable as the next CEO than a better-qualified outsider.	Provide training for the next generation of family leaders in relation to useful skills that will help them grow into a management role. Advise on employment policies that promote the interests of family members over non-family in relation to senior roles.

This is all very challenging, as goal setting is supposed to be; but one standard way of incentivising and rewarding achievement of goals is though reward.

6. Reward

Sharing risk and reward lies at the heart of teams, as summed up in various aphorisms: "Win together, lose together", "There is no 'I' in team", "The whole is greater than the sum of the parts" and many, many more. Reward as an incentive to encourage desired behaviours that contribute towards achieving agreed goals is another accepted tool of management. Therefore, it seems that a team bonus based on achieving the agreed goals that promote the shared purpose would give all advisers an incentive to collaborate.

Something as simple as this should be uncontroversial among advisers who will be familiar with the argument that family businesses need to incentivise their employees even to the extent of families sharing the rewards of ownership. The case in favour of bonuses and sharing ownership encompasses everything from what constitutes fair reward for creating value to the benefits of aligning the interests of employees with the family owners. Reward is the best way of achieving alignment because otherwise, so the argument goes, employees (or advisers) are likely to act in their self-interest and may be tempted to enrich themselves at the expense of the family and its business.

If a family business believes that it stands to gain from cooperation rather than competition among its advisers, a team bonus seems to make sense. In the logic of structuring bonuses, it is common for a proportion of a bonus to be deferred so that the long-term contribution to achieving the shared purpose can be measured and rewarded. This may include the deferred element being forfeited if someone leaves the team before the end of the period of deferral.

This bonus arrangement, however, could conflict with how the adviser is rewarded by his or her host organisation. An adviser whose remuneration is based on individual annual financial performance in terms of fees or commission might be tempted to cheat on the team and do whatever produces more income for him or her, especially if any deferred bonus from pursuing the shared purpose of the family business could take longer to be earned. The adviser who takes this course might lose his or her position on the team and suffer reputational damage; but maybe what matters more for him or her is the short-term remuneration package.

The counterargument to the idea of a team bonus is that promoting group cooperation through this method may be to the detriment of the family business because it will encourage collusion among advisers. The gap in knowledge and information between a family business and

"The best way to hold a team of advisers accountable is to start with what counts for the family business and then find a way to count it."

advisers provides too much opportunity and temptation for advisers to promote their collective self-interest over the interests of the family business. If this is accepted as a persuasive explanation of the motivation of advisers who claim they want to be trusted, the argument continues that if each adviser were encouraged to pursue his or her private interests and to outdo or undermine other team members, this competitive behaviour would produce a better return for the family and its business than would be achieved by a team bonus.

Where does the notion of trust stand in this debate? If it is accepted that trust implies mutual obligations among advisers and between each of them and the family, then this surely must include each of these parties not undermining the interests of the others. A duty of good faith, in simple parlance, is the duty to look out for each other and not to pursue self-interest at the expense of either another team member or the family and its business. This obligation could be based on pure altruism among advisers, or it could be reinforced by a team bonus that supports and rewards this type of behaviour.

This provides three different views on the topic of paying the advisory team a bonus:

- Some would argue that a trusted adviser is one who will act altruistically in the client's best interests without any expectation of reward or recognition. For them, the idea of a team bonus that rewards doing what is morally correct could feel demeaning.
- Others would feel that a team bonus reinforces this moral behaviour through reward.
- The final group would decry any form of shared team reward and argue that the family business receives the best service when advisers individually pursue their respective self-interest, even if this involves members of the team competing with each other.

The self-styled realists, or pessimists, mentioned earlier in this chapter would be in the third camp and would argue that it is now an accepted fact of human behaviour that advisers are motivated by the pursuit of personal interests, no matter how much they claim a client-centric approach in their marketing. These advisers would probably turn the idea of a team bonus against itself to argue that this is an acknowledgment that without a financial incentive, advisers cannot be trusted to pursue the best interests of the family and its business.

In contrast, those who approach being an adviser with a sense of high moral purpose might respond to the realists that the best way to encourage the better side of human nature would be to avoid a team bonus and rely on everyone playing fair. Those in the middle, who might be called pragmatists, would probably endorse this moral view in principle, but agree that some form of team-wide reward should help advisers to stay in lane in terms of their respective contributions to achieving the shared purpose and the overall success of the team.

7. Leadership

If the process of developing an advisory team has been persuasive so far, then the following aspects of leadership have already been addressed:

- The team has a clear sense of the family business's shared purpose and goals have been agreed that clarify what is expected of each adviser on the team. There is no need for a team leader to do this.
- Each team member expects to be held accountable by his or her peers as well as by the family business, and it is unnecessary for individual performances and contributions to be appraised by a team leader.
- Team members have been selected using a set of characteristics and attributes that are designed for working in a team environment and, again, there is no need for a leader to select the team.

This leaves transactional leadership, which must surely be shared among the team and transferred depending on the matters being dealt with at any time. If there is a property to buy or investments to make, or if an employee incentive scheme is desired, the adviser with the relevant specialism will be in charge of leading the team of advisers whose expertise is needed to complete the task in hand. In doing this, all team members accept that the goal of leadership at all levels is team performance as well as individual performance.

8. Family advisers' constitution

Is this type of team desirable, let alone possible?

The client-centric way to frame the question is: what type of team do family businesses want and need? If the answer is an inter-disciplinary group of advisers that thinks and works like a high-performance team, the question becomes: are advisers willing and able to do what is necessary to deliver? The tools for creating a high-performing team mentioned above are not new; it is just their application to a group of professional advisers from different organisations who work for the same family business that seems to be novel. Regulatory constraints might pose some challenges – for example, in relation to team members sharing information with each other or if any team bonuses are treated as tantamount to sharing profits – but the main obstacle to creating this form of inter-disciplinary team could be the attitude of advisers.

"The tools for creating a high-performing team are not new; it is their application to a group of advisers who work for the same family business that is novel."

Might they worry that one of them will cheat on the others and not abide by the rules of the team? If that sounds like a reasonable concern, then one might ask that if a team of advisers with different specialisms and from different organisations find it difficult to trust each other, why do any of them expect to be trusted by the family business which they serve? However, if basing the relationship among a team of advisers on trust alone feels too risky, then maybe the advisers should do what they advise families to do in similar circumstances: write down the rules of the team in a new type of family advisers' constitution. This could be a set of guidelines that are reflected in the engagement letters of the different advisers or a more formal service-level agreement which clearly sets out particular aspects of the service, such as quality, availability and the agreed goals and responsibilities of each team member.

9. Do advisers want to work as a team?

Ultimately, family businesses will need convincing that the model of an advisory team can work cost effectively and generate value that is greater than the sum of its parts. The host organisations of different advisers will need convincing too, so that they do not set incompatible goals that inadvertently punish advisers for focusing on the needs of the team instead of their individual financial performance as measured in their respective organisations.

It is to be expected that some advisers will challenge the distinction made earlier between the familiar multi-disciplinary team and the type of inter-disciplinary team described above. This resistance to changing the established order is similar to the reaction of a family business that is going through succession planning to suggestions from its adviser that it needs to change the way in which the business is owned, led or managed. Advisers will be familiar with family businesses that resist or reject advice that they need to change their established ways, which should serve as a reminder to advisers that many of us naturally tend towards defending the status quo because of its familiarity.

To repeat the quote from Galbraith that was included in the chapter entitled "Do not trust best practices":

> *Numerous factors contribute to the acceptability of ideas. To a very large extent, of course, we associate truth with convenience – with what most closely accords with self-interest and individual well-being or promises best to avoid awkward effort or unwelcome dislocation of life. ... But perhaps most important of all, people approve most of what they best understand. ... Therefore we adhere, as though to a raft, to those ideas which represent our understanding. This is a prime manifestation of vested interest. For a vested interest in understanding is more preciously guarded*

"Advisers need to decide whether they can afford to wait and see whether demand among families for a new type of advisory team builds; and when change eventually happens, hope it will not be too late for them to make the necessary changes to work in this new environment."

> *than any other treasure. It is why men react, not infrequently with something akin to religious passion, to the defence of what they have so laboriously learned. Familiarity may breed contempt in some areas of human behaviour, but in the field of social ideas it is the touchstone of acceptability.*

Amid widespread debates about the inevitability of disruption and change among the professions, it is necessary, in the interests of balance, to offer a defence of the status quo. The well-known arguments for not changing the existing type of advisory team may be summarised as follows:

- Many advisers to family businesses provide an excellent service in line with current practice.
- Change must be demand led and family businesses are not demanding this type of inter-disciplinary team.
- Other advisers are not working as high-performance, inter-disciplinary teams, so there is no pressure from competitors to drive change.
- It is difficult for new approaches to advising family businesses to gain traction in the marketplace and these high barriers to entry make it easier to persist with current practice.
- The costs of change are too high for advisers.

Advisers need to decide whether they can afford to wait and see whether demand among families for a new type of advisory team builds; and when change eventually happens, hope it will not then be too late for them to make the changes that are necessary to work in this new environment. Readers need to form their own views and consider whether changing how a team of advisers works with a family business is desirable at the moment or whether it can be resisted until such time as it is demanded. In the meantime, advisers might find it reassuring to compare the best of current practice with the worst of what changing to a team model might bring, which is another well-known technique for arguing against change.

For every adviser to family businesses who wants to be truly client-centric, and for every family business that seeks superior returns on its investment in advisers, the way forward towards creating a trusted team of advisers is bound to be challenging and interesting. It was ever thus.

About the author

Ken McCracken

Ken McCracken is recognised as one of the leading family business consultants in Europe. His work focuses on helping family businesses and family offices to create the type of governance that will help them to achieve their version of success. He is also actively involved in advocacy to improve the overall awareness of the economic and social contribution made by enterprising families. He a fellow of the Family Firm Institute (FFI), the leading international organisation for family business professionals and academics, and is the author and teacher of the Advanced Certificate in Family Business Advising for the Society of Trust and Estate Practitioners (STEP). He is a past recipient of the FFI Award for Outstanding Interdisciplinary Achievement and the STEP Award for Family Business Adviser of the Year.

www.ingramcontent.com/pod-product-compliance
Ingram Content Group UK Ltd.
Pitfield, Milton Keynes, MK11 3LW, UK
UKHW051823010925
462478UK00006B/66

9 781787 422209